English Glosses
from
British Library
Additional Manuscript
37075

307
310

Hoc uber, -ris, a pappe
Hec mamma, -e, idem
Hoc pectus, -ris, a breste
Hoc latus, -ris, a syde
Hec costa, -e, a rybbe
Hec crates, -is, a sthage
Hoc femur, -ris
Hoc crus, a thye
Hoc veretrum, a pyntyll
Hec pintalonda, -e, idem
Hic testiculus, -i
Hoc genitale, a ballok
Hec piga, -e, a ballokkod
Hic anus, -i, an ars
Hic culus, idem
Hec scanacina, -e, a stale
Hic poples, -tis, a hamme
Hec matrix, -cis, a wombe
in qua generatur infans
Hec vulva, -e, idem
Hoc viscus, -ris, a bowelle
Hoc intestinum, idem
Hoc extum, idem
Hoc septum, -ti, a trype
Hoc diafragma, -tis, a mydrefe
Hec pulpa, -e, for the brawnde
Hoc epar, -tis, a lyver
Hic splen, -is, a mylte
Hoc cor, -dis, a herte

Hic pulmo, -nis, for a longe
Hoc iecur, -ris, a mawe
Hic ren, -nis, a kydney
Hoc cadaver, -ris, for caryone
Hoc umbulicum, a nowlle
Hoc cepum, -i, for talow
Hoc abdomen, -is, for gresse
Hec pinguedo, -is, for fattnes
Hec adeps, -pis, idem
Hoc sumen, idem
Hic sanguis, -nis
Hic cruor, -ris, for blode
Hec omesta for mysyponne
Hoc fel, -is, for a galle
Hec urina, -e, a pyssynge
Urina volat, urina natat, set urina le-
allat
Hoc stercus, -ris, a torde
Hec merda, a terdyll
Hec merdula, parva merda
Hic gibbus, for a tyrtte
Hoc genu, indeclinabile, a knee
Hec tibia, -e, a legge
Hoc internodium, the kne bone
Hec sura, -e, a schynne
Hic limus, -mi
Hic nervus, -i, a synewe
Hec vena, a veyne
Hoc os, ossis, a bone

Folio 310A

ENGLISH GLOSSES
from
BRITISH LIBRARY
ADDITIONAL MANUSCRIPT
37075

Edited, with Notes and Commentary,

by

Thomas W. Ross

and

Edward Brooks, Jr.

Pilgrim Books
Norman, Oklahoma

By Thomas W. Ross
and
Edward Brooks, Jr.

Library of Congress Cataloging in Publication Data

English glosses from British Library Additional Manuscript 37075.
Text in English and Latin.
Includes bibliography and index.
1. English language—Middle English, 1100-1500—Glossaries, vocabularies, etc. 2. Latin language, Medieval and modern—Dictionaries—English. I. Ross, Thomas Wynne, 1923- II. Brooks, Edward. III. British Library. Manuscript. Additional 37075.
PE681.L3E5 1984 423 84-18877
ISBN 0-937664-66-9

Published by Pilgrim Books
P.O. Box 2399, Norman, Oklahoma 73070

ISBN: 0-937664-66-9

CONTENTS

PREFACE

To present the material from British Library Additional Manuscript 37075 in the most useful form, entries have been shortened and brevigraphs, both in Latin and in English, expanded silently. A typical entry includes the Latin article, Latin principal parts or sample grammatical forms, and the English article, often preceded by *for*. This material is usually omitted here. If the omitted material throws light upon the meaning(s) of the English word, a bracketed comment calls that fact to the reader's attention. Thus the complete form of the first entry is "**hoc os, -ris, -i;** for a mouth," which in this edition becomes "**os,** mouth."

Spellings of both English and Latin are retained, even though there are sometimes obvious misspellings (duly noted after the entry). The letters yogh (ȝ) and thorn (þ) are retained, though they occur rarely. Capitals are transcribed as lower-case letters unless there is some reason that they should be retained.

Principal authorities for Latin readings are *A New Latin Dictionary*, ed. Charlton T. Lewis and Charles Short (New York: American Book Co., 1907), and R. E. Latham, *Revised Medieval Latin Word List, from British and Irish Sources* (London: Oxford University Press, 1965); for the English, the *Middle English Dictionary* (*MED*), ed. Hans Kurath et al. (Ann Arbor: University of Michigan Press, 1954–) now complete through the letter *o*; and for the rest of the alphabet the *Oxford English Dictionary*, ed. J. A. Murray et al. (Oxford: Clarendon Press, 1888–1928; *Supplement*, 1933). For the latter, citations are usually provided without subdivision, to avoid unnecessary clutter in the notes.

The Latin is often manifestly incorrect or confused. No attempt has been made to correct it, but when the traditional or classical form of a Latin word provides information about the meaning of the English, this fact is noted.

Editors' conjectural readings are enclosed in square brackets within or following the lemmata. The scribe attempts a rough alphabetical order for some of his material (e.g., on folios 144a ff.). These alphabetical entries occasionally have sub-entries of conceptually related material, not in alphabetical sequence. These are designated by the word *sub-entry* in square brackets.

Folios 302 to 307a are bound out of order. In this edition the order of the leaves in the manuscript is retained, and no attempt to reorganize them has been made. The misbound folios appear in the following order: 302a, 303b, 304a, 302b, 303a, 305b, 306a, 304b, 305a, 307a.

The edition is in two parts: first, the annotated transcription of the English glosses and then an alphabetical index of the English words and phrases, which also includes proper names mentioned in the bracketed commentary.

We would like to express our thanks to Paul G. Ruggiers, of the University of Oklahoma; to Linda Ehrsam Voigts, of the University of Missouri (Kansas City); to Morris L. Cohen, Librarian, Harvard Law School Library; and to the British Library for permission to publish the material from Additional Manuscript 37075.

Colorado Springs, Colorado Thomas W. Ross
Saint Paul, Minnesota Edward Brooks, Jr.

INTRODUCTION

Nominales are lists of Latin words with glosses in one of the vulgar tongues. They were used throughout Europe in the later Middle Ages, and no doubt before as well, as a means of instructing the young in Latin grammar. The Latin is of importance in that it throws light upon the senses and nuances of meaning of the English words. But our interest is in the English. Hence our concern is the converse of that of the Latin master who in the last quarter of the fifteenth century used this collection of instructional devices to educate budding clerks.

Ad (the sigil which we use for the manuscript) exhibits many parallels with other *nominales* of the same period, e.g., the *Promptorium parvulorum*.[1] But it also contains many English words not found elsewhere, either in medieval collections or in the major lexicographical sources, the *Oxford English Dictionary* (*OED*) or the *Middle English Dictionary* (*MED*). Ad is thus a repository of lexical information of some importance, since it not only provides us with a record of otherwise unrecorded words but also often gives a broad range of meanings, or nuances of meaning, through the Latin words that the English terms are intended to gloss.

Though collections like this one were copied from one another (and we do not know the ultimate original), the scribes had the liberty of including from their exemplars only what they thought would be useful, and they could add materials as well. For instance, *paddystolys* (*toadstools,* folio 102a) as a gloss of *boletus* was probably the scribe's own term, not recorded elsewhere, but one that he could confidently expect at least most of his readers or listeners to understand.

How did the lexicographers miss terms like *paddystolys*? Probably any edition of a hitherto unprinted collection of glosses would turn up a similar number of unrecorded words. We cannot conclude, however, that omission from a modern dictionary means that the word was rare, a nonceword, or a *hapax legomenon*. Because such collections were intended for groups of schoolboys, it would not be in the compilers' interests to include outré terms that would baffle their readers.

Ad is composed of 385 paper leaves with outer leaves of vellum and is dated the last quarter of the fifteenth century. A gathering, except for two vellum leaves, is lost at the beginning. Evidently all of its material was collected to serve as a massive manual of instruction, together with some extensive Latin examples. The British Library cataloguer who first described the manuscript in 1907 distinguished forty items. Many of these Latin works are to be found in other manuscripts and have been made available in modern editions—for example, the Latin lines beginning *Stans puer ad mensam* (folios 22a–23a); the *Facetus* (folios 52b–58a) sometimes attributed to Cato and more recently to John of Garland; verses on gender from the *Doctrinale* of Alexander de Villa Dei (folios 58b-69b); a collection of synonyms, again sometimes attributed to John of Garland or to Matthieu de Vendôme or John of Garland and published in Migne, *PL* 150, col. 1577 (folios 97b–114a); the so-called *Distichs of Cato* (folios 199a–204b); a treatise on figures of speech with verses from the *Doctrinale* (see above) on folios 225b–34b and then continued on folios 355a–59b; the *Liber parabolarum* of Alanus de Insulis, published in Migne, *PL*, 210, col. 581 (folios 245a–55b); an incomplete hymnal (folios 362a–81b); and an incomplete collection of sequences (folios 382a–end).[2] The only English items from Ad that have been published are the proverbs and their Latin equivalents on folios 70a–71a.[3] I have also abstracted some glosses as part of the material for an article.[4]

But the great bulk of Ad has never been printed—and has probably seldom been read in its entirety during the last four or five centuries. The present edition includes only the English glosses, with their Latin equivalents, which are, of course, most useful in determining meanings and shades of meaning. We have omitted items that are entirely in Latin, without English commentary. One of these, the treatise on rhetoric (folios 355a–59b) might be of interest to literary historians concerned with late-medieval Latin, since it includes examples from classical writers like Tully (Cicero) and mentions Homer, whose works were not known in the Middle Ages but whose name was venerated. However, most of this material is already available in good modern studies and editions.[5]

Two major English items in Ad are the series of glosses that begin "Os, facies, mentum" (folios 7aff.) and the *Nominale* (folios 309ff.). These appear to be in the same scribal hand. Other items in Ad are in different hands, but all are from the late fifteenth century.

There is no certain indication of provenance. The British Museum cataloguer thought that the volume had been the property of a London schoolboy,[6] but it seems more likely that it was once in the possession of a master who used it to teach his pupils. Books were, of course, expensive, and this fact, together with the presence of some of the sophisticated Latin material in the collection, makes it seem more probable that the book belonged to an older owner. London as a provenance is suggested by a description on folio 191a of rose garlands prepared to celebrate Saint Anthony's Day ("in sancti antonij solennitate"). Saint Anthony's School in Threadneedle Street, in London, might well have been the institution where the instruction book was used. At about the time that Ad was assembled, young Thomas More was a pupil at this school.

On folio 192b occurs a pair of Latin sentences in which the speaker, a young scholar, says that after learning grammar in London he expects to move either to Cambridge or to Oxford to continue his studies. However, this pair of sentences is part of a series of exercises (apparently a sentence composed by the master, another composed by the scholar, both translating the same English phrases) and therefore cannot be regarded as wholly trustworthy evidence of provenance. On folio 204b at the conclusion of the *Distichs of Cato* appears "a Warrewyke," which suggests that at least a portion of the manuscript was copied there. Further, on folio 168a in a paragraph explaining adverbs of time there occurs "tunc fui cantuarie" which, of course, might indicate Canterbury as a place of origin but might just as well be a place-name chosen at random to illustrate the inflection of the locative case.

The dialect of the English glosses appears to be Southeast Midland. On folios 25b and 52a occurs the name Clavering, a noted North Country family; the signature is in a fifteenth-century hand. This happenstance might explain the occurrence of the Northern *a* for Southeast Midland *o* in a word like *drane* (folios 13b, 315b); however, this dialectical feature is of too rare occurrence to be given much weight. It might be a scribal whim.

The English words in Ad provide a window through which one might hope to glimpse something of the life in England about 1475–1500. The historian of manners and customs is tempted to extrapolate from the presence of certain terms or classes of terms. One must be cautious about drawing conclusions from these data. The "window" may be a darkened glass. Much of the Latin and English was copied from an earlier manuscript, which in turn was copied from another, and so on. Thus the collection of terms might represent an earlier stratum of experience.

On the other hand, although the scribes of Ad no doubt tried to copy the lists of Latin words accurately, they would not transcribe an unfamiliar English gloss or one that reflected an obsolete sense or pronunciation. We may assume, then, that the English in Ad is the familiar language of about 1475.

Through this glass, darkly, we may see something of late-medieval life, particularly that of the schoolmaster and schoolboy. Though the school where Ad was used may have been in London, the countryside was near at hand, as the great number of terms for plants, trees, and animals would seem to indicate. The richness and breadth of English daily living are surely indicated by the variety of dwellings, furniture, clothing, professions, and trades. Naturally enough, given the nature of common-school education, of its masters and its scholars, there is a bright focus upon religious life, its accouterments, and the officers of its church.

There are frequent references to torture and pain, but at the same time there are the lively catalogues of musical forms and instruments; of terms connected with bookmaking, including the illuminator (*limner*) and the binder; of jewelry and the appurtenances of the lady's toilette. There are lists of weapons and machines of battle, but the gentler crafts of baking and spinning are not forgotten.

The presence—the unabashed presence—of words that have since become taboo should not surprise those who have read Chaucer, Dunbar, or the secular lyrics of the age. Farting, pissing, and ass holes are as much a part of the life reflected in Ad as are the terms for church architecture.

Since most schoolmasters were in holy orders, as were most scribes, the lists of ecclesiastical terms are not surprising. Reflected here is a world in which breviaries and albs play an important part, but so too do taverns, business dealings, and food in astonishing variety.

The first of the systematic glosses begins, however, with the human body; this focus upon man is perhaps significant, in a modest way, of a nascent humanism or at least of a man-centered culture. The list of body parts is almost clinical in its inclusiveness. Evidently it was thought necessary for schoolboys to know the Latin names not only for their arms and legs but also for internal organs and other intimate parts. Some of the young clerks might well have become physicians.

A half dozen other examples of the English words not to be found in the *OED* or the *MED* indicate something of the range of the unique words in Ad: *messelyne*, folio 16a; *trefolde*, folio 61b; *wakabul*, folio 62a; *borowe*, folio 65a; *mantyll*, folio 66a; and *maindyr*, folio 66b. Sometimes the lexicographers have missed the word altogether (e.g., *trefolde*, folio 61b). At other times they have recorded the term but from later documentary sources (e.g., *mantyll*, folio 66a); or they have recorded different senses for a word (e.g., *borowe*, folio 65a).

Though, as stated above, Ad was probably a schoolmaster's property, it may have been lent to one of his pupils at one time or another. Someone announces, "I haue fownd a snakys skyne" (folio 275b), which sounds as if a schoolboy is making a delighted proclamation of discovery, through this note, to one of his fellows—perhaps during a time when talking was forbidden.

Folio 323b has two naughty (schoolboy?) annotations, added interlinearly. The collocation of suggestive terms on this leaf (*pyntil*, *arse lyke*, *breche*, *love*, and *the dewyll*) may be coincidental, but one might surmise that the presence of *breche*, *love*, and *the dewyll* in the text itself led (or misled) some adolescent annotator or glossator to add his own *pyntil* and *arse lyke*. The occurrence on folio 244a of the clever but naughty macaronic verses which are a homosexual invitation may provide further evidence of the sexual situation that is sometimes to be found in all-male groups in prisons—or boys' schools.

Although some of the all-Latin pieces in Ad indicate that the owner, user, or reader had some intellectual pretensions, the linguistic level of the Latin-English glosses is not high. The Latin is often garbled, misunderstood, or erratically spelled—evidence of corruption that is surprising even in the days of late-medieval decadent Latin. For instance, the scribe records *paster* for *passer* (folio 20b), *velus* for *vetus* (folio 110a), *auibio* for *auidio* (folio 142b), *siluerestris* for *siluestris* (folio 165a), and *caus* for *casus* (folio 173b).

Clearly, and understandably, the scribes were more at home in English, but they had problems even with their native language. Some of these were the result of shortcomings endemic to scribes as a class. For instance, *casa* for *case* (folio 19b) may be the result of eye skip, since the next entry, *cirotica*, ends in *-a*. Similarly, *bowbyll* for *dowbyll* (folio 21a) may have been caused by the proximity of the initial *b-* in *biuium*, the Latin word that it glosses. The error *the powntyd* for *thre powntyd* (*three-pointed*, folio 66b) is the kind of mistake any of us might commit, writing the familiar *the* for the less common *thre*. Similarly there are frequent confusions of two similar words, resulting in misspellings like *hold* for *hole* on folio 65b, though this particular scribal slip may also have been caused by the similarity of the letters *d* and *e* in late-fifteenth-century hands.

One is naturally curious to determine how a collection like that in Ad was used. Rote memory played a large part. Though the master may have lent his copy to one of his pupils, it usually remained in his possession. One may plausibly imagine the master dictating the Latin and each boy in turn reciting the English meaning, or, alternatively, the master reading the English, the pupil responding in Latin. Perhaps each scholar had his own slate or wax tablet to record the wisdom from the instructor and from Ad.

The material is arranged in two ways: first, ideational categories (e.g., body parts), a rudimentary way of presenting material in a foreign tongue; second, grammatical categories (e.g., deponent verbs), which demand more linguistic sophistication but are admittedly a deadly dull way to teach. But we are forced to imagine scores of English schoolboys learning such lists by heart. Mistakes were punished by a *ferula*, a blow on the hand (see fol. 305b). We recall that in Joyce's *A Portrait of the Artist* Stephen Dedalus is (wrongfully) punished in the same way, with what Irish schoolboys called a *pandy*.

The compendium in Ad gives no clue to the socioeconomic group that produced the students. Indeed, specialists in fifteenth-century history and education seem to have few data about this important matter. We do know, however, that Eton had a special provision to give "free instruction in grammar to all comers."[7] It has been claimed that "in the fifteenth century, no person of any rank or station above merely labouring men seems to have been wholly illiterate," but such estimates are probably exaggerated.[8] On the other hand, the century did indeed mark the foundation of many schools in London and elsewhere in England, including Eton, Magdalen College School, Ewelme, and Rotherham. A. F. Leach, an authority on English education in the later Middle Ages, discovered that of the thirty-three guilds that he studied twenty-eight maintained grammar schools. In 1447 the Commons petitioned for an additional four schools in the City of London and spoke of the "grete nombre of gramer scholes" in the realm, besides those in London. Furthermore, a common meritorious act was to endow a chantry which required not only that the priest say daily masses for his benefactor's soul but that he also keep a school. Not all education was in the hands of the clergy (though most of it was); in fact, there was the stipulation that the master of one grammar-school should be "in sacris ordinibus minime constitutus" ("not in holy orders at all").[9]

Since schools proliferated during these troubled times, we should anticipate the proliferation of collections like those in Ad, the *Promptorium*, and other such manuscripts. On the other hand, the same kinds of instruction books were doubtless used in preceding centuries as well. And it may be merely the relative recentness of these fifteenth-century manuscripts that accounts for their survival in such numbers. "Tempus edax rerum" and likewise "tempus edax librorum": fire, theft, use and abuse, together with dripping ceilings and noses, make the scarcity and actual disappearance of earlier medieval manuscripts a sad but familiar phenomenon.

The contents of British Library Additional Manuscript 37075 have no literary value. However, its mass of material, much of it not recorded elsewhere, provides information about the nature of English during that period when what we label "Middle English" was slowly and subtly changing into the modern language. The scribes' wayward spelling habits are evidence of the decay of older inflections (e.g., *-n* for infinitives as in *caste, castyn*, folios 145a, 165b, 334a) and sounds (e.g., the voiceless velar fricative as in *fyȝthe*, *fytyn*, folios 129a, 338a).

Furthermore, the glosses provide information about the meanings of hundreds of words that must be understood so that one can more sensitively interpret both earlier and later literary texts, including Chaucer and Shakespeare. Thus it may be argued that Ad does have indirect literary significance.

The Latin in Ad, especially the sometimes lengthy lists of synonyms, supplies nuances and multiplicities of meaning that supplement the information already available in the great dictionaries. This edition thus provides a modest increment in our understanding of the language spoken and written five hundred years ago, in the transitional period between Middle and Early Modern English.

T.W.R.

INTRODUCTORY NOTE

Thomas W. Ross suggested that he and I might together prepare this edition. There are differences in our approach to the material and in the points that we have emphasized, as one would expect in an enterprise such as this. As a Latinist, I am most at home in works of classical antiquity, and I have had to beware of confounding the ancient meaning of a Latin word with the sense it assumed in this late-fifteenth-century compilation. Despite the misspellings and corruptions of many sorts that occur in the Latin of this manuscript, I have tried not to forget Quintilian's denunciation of those foolhardy editors who "*dum librariorum insectari volunt inscientiam suam confitentur*" ("reveal their ignorance while inveighing against scribes"). I have indicated the classical equivalent of a Latin word only when such an addition sheds light on the English. As a Latinist, I have many times had to resist the temptation to cite words and phrases of such early etymologists and compilers as Varro and Isidore and to produce excursuses on the origin of such terms as *speculum*, *augur*, *ampullor*, and *histrionor*.

E.B.

ENGLISH GLOSSES

Folio 7a

[Each group of glosses is preceded by a summary list of Latin words. For similar lists, see those beginning on fols. 292a and 309a.]

os, mouth [first line partly illegible owing to stain]
facies, face
mentum, chyne
dens, tothe
guttur, throte
lingua, tonge
palatum, rofe of the mowth
barba, berde
supercilium, vpper browe
silium, the nether browe
frons, forhede
tempora, tempill
labrum, lippe
palpebra, ye lidd
acies, þe ye sight of the y [*ye* added above]
oculus, ye
albugo, the white of the ye
pupilla, the balle of the ye
purila, the cop of the nose [*cop*, tip]
pus, the fylth of the nose
nasus, nose
interfinium, the space withyn the nose
naris, the grystill of the nose

Folio 7b

sinciput, the for[e]parte of the hede
intersiput, the myddil part of the hede
occiput, the hynder part of the hede
cerebrum, brayne
pars, parte
caput, hede
cranium, brayne pan
vortex, noddill
discrimen, shed of the here
aurus, ere
faux, cheke
iungiua, gumme [of the mouth; *iungiua, gingiva*]
frontenella, nek pytt
capillus, here
cartilago, grystil bone
legia, ere lappe
genninus, cheke toth
palma, pame of the hond
iunctura, ioynte
manus, honde
vlna, met yerde [yard, three feet]
lacertus, fadym

Folio 8a

vnguis, nayle
digitus, fynger
humerus, shulder
pectus, brest
collum, nek
acella, arme pytt
pugnus, fyste
cubitus, elbowe
sanguis, blode
mamma, pappe
venter, wombe
vesica, bladdyr

tergum, bak
spondile, bakbone
costa, rybbe
vmbelicus, navyll
latus, syde
caro, flessh
pellis, skynne
nates, buttok

Folio 8b

cor, harte
splen, mylte
pulmo, lownge
lien, longe [repeated by error; *lien*, milt or spleen]
fel, galle
ren, kedney
diafragma, mydryfe
iecur, mawe [belly; however, *jecur*, liver]
arteria, gret pype
stomacus, stomok
intestinum, gutt bowell
epar, liuer [*epar*, *hepar*]
anus, arse
crus, thye
pubes, schare [division or fork of the body; pubic region, groin; *pubes*, corr. from *pubeis*]
dorsum, bake
spina, bakebone
podex, arse hole
vertebra, whyrll bone [vertebra]
genu, kne
internodium, knepane
naruis, senewe
poples, ham [ham of the knee]
sura, chyn [shin; *sura*, calf]

Folio 9a

[Two illegible lines]
musculus, þe calffe of þe legge
vena, vayne
tibia, legge
sophena, mastir vayne
articulus, too
planta, sole of þe foote
calix, hele
medulla, mari [marrow]
cavilla, splent bone
callus, pathe [out of place, distinguishing *callus* from *callis*]
callis, þe harnesse [error for *hardnesse*; *MED*, *hardnesse*, 1. (c), a callous] of þe fote
allus, a grette too
pollex, thombe [repeated by error]
index, schewing fynger
medius, þe middill fynger
medicus, a leche fynger [traditional for fourth finger; *leche*, physician, who evidently used the fourth finger for examination]
auricularis, þe lytill fynger [*auricularis* indicates that the little finger was used to clean the ear]

Folio 9b

[Two illegible lines]
panis, brede
ceruisia, ale
cocliar, spone
sall, salte
sepe, onyn [onion; altered from *a*-]
mappa, cloyth
discus, dysch
puls, potege
olus, wurtys
legimine, growell
faba, a benee [error for *bene*]
pisa, pese
os, bone
caro, flesch
salsa, sawce
pissis, fisch
allec, heringe [*allec*, *alec*, fish brine]
ouum, egke
farculum, messe of mette
fragmentum, brokyn mette
lac, milke

Folio 10a

[One illegible line]
[Illegible], chese
butirum, butture
artocapus, simle [*simnel,* bread made with fine flour]
libum, wastell [fine bread]
colophium, bonne [bun]
vipa, wyne soppe, watyr soppe
flaton, flawane [flan, a kind of pie or cake]
gingiberum, gynger
piper, pepper
allium, garlyk
sinapium, musterd
acetum, eysell
assa, rost
crocus, safroun
succus, iouse [juice]
pastillus, pastey
cuminum, commyn
cultellus, knyfe

Folio 10b

[One or two lines illegible]
pomum, appille
ciphus, cupp
vinum, wyne
mensa, tabill
tripos, trestillis
lauacrum, lavyr [laver, ewer (to wash hands)]
peluis, basoun
manitergium, towell
vitrum, glasse
pertica, perche [linear measure, ten rods]
cathedra, cheyre
puluinum, quysshene [cushion]
auis, byrde
catesta, cage
ipopurgium, awndirene [andiron; *ipopurgium* approximates *hypopodium*]
follis, belowe
scamnum, benche

Folio 11a

[One line illegible]
scabellium, stole
alea, the dice
scaccarium, the chessboard
scaccus, chessmane
talus, a dice
purgus, poyt [error for *poynt; purgus,* error for punctus? *OED* , point, 21, one of the squares of a chessboard]
fex, fylth
calathus, paner [pannier]
cadus, barell
onoforus, costrell [flask, bottle]
clipsedra, spygett
corbis, lepe [basket]
dolium, tonne
nectar, swete wyne
mustum, mustum [error for *must,* new wine]
obba, bottell
teca, cace
ignis, fyre

Folio 11b

[Two lines illegible]
fumus, smoke
fax, bronde
gleba, turfe
fauilla, sparkyll
cratis, gredeyrene [gridiron]
contus, posstyk [stick for beating clothes; *OED, poss,* v., 3, to beat clothes in water with a heavy pestle-like instrument; first cit., 1611]
olla, potte
patella, panne
creagra, fleshoke [fleshhook]
parapsis, dysche
lixa, kychyne page
tripos, trivet
situla, boket
cacabus, cawderne [cauldron]

sartago, fryng panne [*fryng*, error for *fryyng*]
spatula, sklyce [*OED*, *slice*, sb.[1], 4, spatula; records sp. *scl-*, *skl-*]
piper, pepir
mola, qwyrne [mill]

Folio 12a

[Two lines illegible]
[flamma], flame
bracte, brechis
camisa, shert
lodex, blanket
linthium, shete
lectus, bede
collobium, tabard
tunica, coote
ma[ni]ce, sleve
pennula, furre
pannus, clothe [cloth]
ceruical, boster [bolster]
madula, iordeyne [jordan, chamber pot]
clauis, key
scrinium, cafyr [coffer; *MED* records no spelling *ca-*]
sera, loke
flamitium, kerchefe [*flamitium*, *flauutium* or *flammium*?]
reticlium, kall [calle, net (for hair)]
triberus, bonet

Folio 12b

[Two lines illegible]
hostium, durre [door]
paries, wall
fenestra, wyndow
area, flowre [floor]
postis, post
solium, sete
camera, chamber
pini, spense [spence, room in which victuals or liquor are stored]
aula, hall
coquina, kychene
perpendiculum, lewell [level]
dolabrum, brde axe [*brde*, error for *brode*]
bipennis, twybyll [two-edged ax]
amussus, sqwyre [square]
assia, an addys [adze]
terebrum, augyr
celtis, chesell
penetrale, pereser [piercer, awl]
assula, chyppe
serra, sawe

Folio 13a

[Two lines illegible]
linea, lyne
creta, chalk
dolo, wegge [wedge, altered from *m-*; *dolo*, staff with sharp iron point]
circinus, compase
apoka, skore [*score*, tally; *apoka* from Gr. *apoché*, receipt]
dica, tayle [tally]
ortus, gardeyn
fons, well
aqua, water
stagnum, pond
pons, bryge
mergo, bruyk [error for *brynk*; *MED*, *brinke*, 1. (b), bank of a stream]
porrum, leke [*leek* (out of place, but see *herbe* below)]
vanga, spade
ligo, mattok
tribula, sholve [error for *shovel*? *tribula*, *tribulue*, caltrop, hence briar]
fimus, donge
furca, forke
herba, herbe

Folio 13b

[Two lines illegible]
palus, myre
sepes, hegge
tribulus, brere
spina, thorne

planta, plant
prunus, plombe tre
cerasus, cheritre
nux, nvtt or nvttre
vlmus, elme
vitis, vyne
vua, grape
fauus, honycombe
apes, bee
cera, wex
mel, hony
apiarium, beehyve
fucus, drane [drone]
arbor, tree
folium, lefe
redix, rote
ramus, bowe
cortex, the barke of a tre

Folio 14a

[One line illegible]
iter, weuey [way]
lapis, stone
sespes, turfe
limus, slyme
puteus, pitte
trocus, toppe [*top* (child's toy); troc(h)us, Gr. *trochós,* ball, hoop, wheel]
pila, ball
discus, dyche or coyte [dish or quoit]
ludus, pley
palestra, wrastlyngplace
domus, hous
ecclesia, chyrche
castrum, castell
murus, wall
casa, cote [cot, cottage]
porta, gate
cereus, tapyr
ara, awter [altar]
gradus, a grece [pl. of *gre,* stair; here perhaps = *gradual* (collection of Psalms; see fols. 299b, 318b]
vitrui, a glasse
crux, crosse
lampa, lampe
imago, image

Folio 14b

[Two lines illegible]
examitum, amise
alba, albe
pixis, boxe
oblata, obley [*MED, oble,* bread or wafer used in the Sacrament]
frola, cruett [small vessel used for sacramental wine]
viaticum, the sacrament
crisma, holy creme
encaustum, ynke
cornu, horne
pumex, pomye [pumice]
regula, rewle [straightedge]
margo, margyn
tumulus, grave
libitina, bere [bier; *libitina,* Venus Libitina, goddess of funeral equipment, corpses]
fons, well
campana, bell
lucerna, lanterne

Folio 15a

[Three lines illegible]
mons, hyll
vallis, valey
ager, felde
via, wey
pratum, medow
flos, flowre
fenum, hey
spica, ere of corne
falx, sythe
granum, corne
merges, shefe
arista, ere
cirpus, ryshe [rush (plant)]
formicentum, pyssmyre hyll
torrens, broke
ripa, bank

agger, heepe
aruum, feld

Folio 15b

[Two lines illegible]
limes, vey [way, path; *limes, limas,* sidelong, aslant; *limitis,* crosspath]
sulcus, forw [furrow]
lira, herpe
vellus, flese [fleece]
agnus, lambe
ouis, shepe
aries, ramme
pellis, skynne
ouile, fo[l]de
cratis, hurdell
bostar, oxestall
vinclum, bond
vincella, shakyll
restis, wythe [withe, to bind animals]
palea, chaffe
vannus, vanne [*OED, van,* sb.[2], winnowing basket or shovel]
arcanius, cokke [haycock]
orreum, barne
far, whete

Folio 16a

[One line illegible]
triturato, thresshre
acus, chaffe
cribum, syffe [sieve]
flagellum, flayle
rastrum, rake
frumentum, whete
sigolum, rye
ordeum, barley
mixtilis, messelyne [not in *MED*; *mixtilis,* Lat. *mastillio,* maslin, mixed corn (especially wheat and rye)]
eruca, carloke [cherlok, wild mustard]
lolium, cokkyll
zizania, darnell
auena, ote
hostorium, a strykyllus [strickle, stick used to level off grain in container]
modius, busshell
stopa, besom [broom]

Folio 16b

[One line illegible]
apoca, score [account, debt]
dica, tayle [tally]
pistrium, bakehous
pasta, paste
furnus, ovyne
farina, mele
plumbum, leed
vsterium, kylne
granomellum, groute [grout, coarse grain]
mola, qwerne [*quern,* mill]
cilicium, an heyre [*MED, here,* n. (2), covering originally made of goat's hair, used by seamen]
nauis, shyppe
rete, nette
mare, the see
remus, ore
velum, seyle

Folio 17a

[One line illegible]
ancora, ankyr
naulum, shypmannas hyre [passage money; *naulum, nallium* in rubric]
rudens, gabyll [cable]
corda, corde
nereus, goode of see [*goode,* God]
axis, extre [axletree]
biga, carte
iugum, yok
radius, spoke
rota, whele
stilio, nathe [*MED, nathe,* nave of a wheel; but *stilio,* felly, rim]
cantus, vtter parte of þe the whele [*the* repeated in error]

aratrum, plowe
vomer, share
cultrum, cultyr
gerusa, goode [goad]

Folio 17b

capistrum, ha[lter]
herpica, harow
falere, harnes
postela, crowper
temo, thyll [wagon shaft]
veredus, thyllhors
aer, eyre
sol, þe sonne
nubes, cloude
iris, reynbowe
luna, mone
stella, sterr
nix, snowe
tonitrus, [English erased; probably *thonder*]
grado, heyle
pluuia, reyne
fulgur, lytenynge
pruina, whorefrost

Folio 18a

[One line illegible]
gelu, frost
turbo, whyrelewynd
glacies, est [error for *yce, ice*]
radius, sonebeeme
calor, heete
estas, somere
scissor, taylour
acus, nedill
filum, threde
forfex, peyre of sheris
digitale, thymbyll
ulna, elne [ell, measure]
corium, ledyr
fibula, a nall [*MED* records sp. *nall* (nail) and *nal* (an awl)]
sotularis, shoe
aluta, cordewane
galla, last

Folio 18b

[One line illegible]
persegmen, p[ersyn]g of ledyr
corrigia, thong
seta, brystyll
intercucium, welt
solea, sole
ansorium, kuttyng knyf
lana, woll
colus, dystaff
fusus, spyndyll
stupa, towe
mataxa, hechyll [instrument for carding flax]
linum, flex
vrcelolus, posnet [small metal pot for boiling; *vrceolus* in rubric]
cune, cradyllis
papatum, pappe [pap, baby food]
fassia, cradyll bonde
latus, brode [broad]

Folio 19a

[Two lines illegible]
sella, sadyll
strepa, styrop
calcar, spurre
frenum, brydyll
capistrium, halter
ocrea, boote
tenia, lappe of the boote
antela, peytrell [breast armor for horse; perhaps only breastband, though *OED* does not include this sense]
mantica, male [pouch]
ferrum, yrene
caliga, hose
ligula, laynayrde [*lainer*, lace, thong, strap]
laqueus, lace
lumbare, pauncherde [armor for lower part of body]

tela, webe
zona, gyrdyll
loculus, purse
acurare, nedyll casa [error for *case*]

Folio 19b

cirotica, a [illegible]
argentum, syluyr
libra, pound
solidus, shyllyng
numisma, the prynt of money
aurum, gold
forceps, tongis
icus, anfeld [anvil; *icus*, error for *incus*]
fabrica, forge
malleus, hamyr
caminus, chymney
calibs, stele
ferrum, yren
frustrum, gobet
camus, barnkyll [*bernacle*, snaffle bit]
metallum, metell
forpex, peyre of sysers
speculum, a glasse
petten, combe

Folio 20a

[One line illegible]
nouacla, rasyr
cos, whetestone
lancea, spere
gladius, swerd
pilum, darte
sagitta, arow
arcus, boowe
bestia, brest [error for *beest*]
volucris, bryd [bird]
serpens, serpent
homo, man
musca, flye
vermis, worme
pullus, foole [foal]
equus, horse
equa, mare
villus, calfe
bos, oxe
vacca, cowe

Folio 20b

taurus, a [bolle]
porcus, hooge
porcellus, pygge
nefrendus, barow hogge [*nefrendus*, lit. toothless]
apis, bore
sus, swyne
gallus, cok
gallina, henne
pullus, chykyne
ancer, gandyr
anca, goos
canis, dogge
catulus, whelpe
sorex, ratt
mureligus, catt
mus, mowse
paster, sparow [*paster*, error for *passer]*
anas, dukke

Folio 21a

aquila, egyll
cornix, crowe
coruus, ravyn
columba, dove
urbs, citee
ciuis, citezene
biuium, dowbyll wey
opella, shoppe
lanista, bocher [butcher]
macellum, shamyllus [shambles, butchershop]
carcer, prisoun
collistrigium, pilery
compes, fetyr
catena, chene
vngule, clawe
cauda, tayle
pilus, heere

cor, herte
tucetum, a poddyngis [*OED*, pudding, 2., entrails (usually pl.)]

Folio 21b

cruor, blode
extum, gutte
Explicit offacies mentum, [*offacies*, error for *os facies*]

Folio 30b

[Contains some English grammatical explanations, beginning: "Ego sum creatura dei þis verbe *sum* ys þe singular nombyr and þe fyrst persoun for so is the nominatyve case *ego* and euery verbe shall acord with the nominatyve case in nombyr and persoun."]

Folio 37a

[Contains some Latin verses, a signature, John Boothe [?], and the date 1682.]

Folio 39a

[Computation of the age of the world: "Frome þe gynnyng of þe worlde to þe incarnacioun of cryst v. M. ij. C. (5200) yeris, saue a yere."]

Folio 44b

[Interlinear glosses, including those below]
experiolus, polle katte
lutricius, otyr
basiliscus, koke a tryce
vipera, addyr
vespe, waspys
siro, handworme [mite (acarid) that burrows in the hand]
oestrum, brese [breeze, gadfly]
culice, gnatt

Folio 45a

tortu, tortes
cicada, grashoper
papilio, boter fly
furone, feret
mordax, erwyg
canis, doge fyche [dogfish]
congrum, congur [conger, eel]
soliam, sole
sanguisaga, watyr leche

Folio 45b

polipis, lopstar [lobster]
lupus, wolfefyche
hesitabit, dowȝt

Folio 52a

[At bottom of folio, signature of John Clavueryng, in a hand contemporary with those of the scribes. He is not in the *DNB* but was perhaps a forebear of his famous namesake, the opponent of Warren Hastings, whose dates are 1722–77. The Claverings were a noted North Country family.]

Folio 58b

[Treatise on the gender of nouns]
leuita, decunn [deacon]
heremita, a narmet [an hermit]
papa, pope

Folio 59a

[Some illegible words]
abatissa, abbas [abbess]
pincerna, boteler
tamisia, temmys [Thames]
pomus, appyll tre
rubus, busche
herba odore fera, wyld comyn [cumin]
nomina propria angelorum, mi-

chaell gabriell

Folio 59b

nomina deorum ydolorum, iuipiter
passer,sparowe
gallus, kok
columbus, male dowfe [dove]
gallina, henne
columba, female dowfe

Folio 60a

musa, muse

Folio 60b

[Two lines illegible]
angligena, englischman
pincerna, boteler
agricola, tyller
francigina, frenchman
lixa, kechynpage
aduena, stranger
domina, lady
ceta. . .balena, whale
muscela, whesyl [weasel]
taspa, molle
dama, doo
pantera, panter [panther]

Folio 61a

mare, þe see
cubile, bede [bed]
vtrumque, euyr edyr [either one; not in *MED*]
phebe, þe mone
pentecoste, whytsontyde
cete, whalis

Folio 61b

gummus, gume
huiusmodi, suche maner
fornudo, a rede [reed? *fornudo*, perhaps error for *arundo*]
imago, ymage
cardo duno, a trefold [triple-folding door? triptych? not in *OED*; *cardo*, hinge, threshold]
mergo, a mergenum [margin; *MED* records no sp. in *-enum*]
ordo, ordyr
exipiuntur prehendo, false
presto, redy
homo, man
nemo, nobody
latro, theff [thief]
proximitas, nynesse [nighness, nearness]

Folio 62a

cornu, horn
lac, mylke
tot, so many
quot, how many
quot quot, how so euermany
tribunal, iustis sete
mel, hony
nil, nowth [nought]
vigill, wakabul [error for *wakeful*? not in *OED*]
pugill, champioun
consull, meyer [mayor]

Folio 62b

presull, byshopp
neganda, cursyd
tantumdem, alsomych [as much as]
totidem, allsomany
nis, kedney
pecteum, combe
splen. . . lien, þe mylt
siren, marmayd
flatus uentri, blast

Folio 63a

delphyn, quidam pissis, delphyn
geralogodium, tryakyl [treacle; medicinal compound, originally a salve]

calcar, spore [spur]
sotulare, schoo [shoe, though *sotulare* suggests shoemaker]
spinter, pyn
inder deris, dunge [dung? *inder deris* provides no clue]
vesper, þe euyn tyde
iuger, a forlong

Folio 63b

[Beginning here, Latin words are arranged according to endings: *-er, -ir,* etc.]
[Illegible], a foteman [Latin dim, perhaps *pedester*]
acer, sowyre, [sour]
celer, swyfte
saluber, holsome
cadauer, caryoun
ymber, showre
mater, modyr
piper, pepyr
cucumer, gowrde
puber, young
vber, plentyfull
deginer, owte of kynde [unnatural]
pauper, pore
linter, shyppe

Folio 64a

vir, man
ir, þe pame of hond
pir, fyre
martir, mertir
memor, myndfull
doctior, wyser
femor, holde
autor, fynder
equor, þe see
marmor, marbull
cor, hert
arbor, tre
soror, sustyr
vxor, wyfe

Folio 64b

discolor, dym color
murmur, grugyng [grudging; complaining]
turtur, tyrtyldowfe [turtledove]
furfur, thefe
augur, wycche

Folio 65a

bonitas, goodnesse
assis, halpeny
vas, borowe [*vas,* pledge, security; *borowe,* burrow, cave; not in *MED*; perhaps *borrow*.]
mas, man
nugas, iapyng
abbas, abbot
borias, þe north wynde
primas, a primet
gigas, put [pit; *gigas,* error for *gurges*?]
nephas, cursydness
vas, vessell
gurges, strem
seges, corne

Folio 65b

compes, peyr of feturs [pair of fetters]
quatripes, a fowr fotyd best
apis, bee
miles, knyȝth
eques, horsman
superstes, a lyue [alive; *superstes,* one who remains alive after another's death]
diues, ryches
ebes, dull
sospes, hold and sownd [whole and sound]
propes, swyfte
teres, rownde
comes, felow
hospes, geest

antistes, byschopp
ales, byrde
proles, chyld
vrres, hoog [*hoog*, altered from *hogg*; *vrres*, properly *verres*]
lebes, cauderyn [cauldron]
dies, day

Folio 66a

meridies, þe mydday
heres, eyr [heir]
locuples, rych
paries, wall
quies, rest
pes, foote
es, brasse
clauis, keye
molaris, mylstone
callis, castell
lapis, stone
pixis, boxe
clamis, mantyll [mantel; not in *MED*; first cit. in *OED*, 1519]
sinis, schyn [shin; *sinis*, error for *cruris*, gen. of *crus*]
orbis, worlde
vnguis, clee [claw]

Folio 66b

[fer]ris, the axis [axis]
pestis, þe penstelens [pestilence]
neptis, nese [niece]
vallis, valey
bipennis, twybyll [two-edged ax]
cassis, helmet
iaspis, a precius stone
restis, wyth [withe, to fetter animals]
aspis, maindyr [not in *MED*; error for *addyr*?]
pell, skyn [altered from *syn*]
turris, tower
vestis, cloth
peluis, bason
cuspis, þe pownt of a knyfe [*pownt*, point]
glis, cley
glis, bur [*glis*, distinguished from foregoing by gen. *glitis*]
finis, end
climis, þe reynys
classis, a navy of shyppys
messis, corne
tussis, the cowth [cough]
ibis, snyte [snite, snipe]
lis, stryfe
triscuspis, the powntyd [error for *thre powntyd* (pointed)]
dicis, rych
testis, wytness
ciuis, cytysyn
burgensis, burgesse
hostis, henmy [enemy]
canis, dog
iuuenis, yong man
scolaris, scoler

Folio 67a

os, mowth
os, bone [*os*, distinguished from foregoing by gen. *ossis*]
caos, chause, dyrknes [darkness; *chause* added above in later hand]
melos, melody
cos, wetston [whetstone]
dos, dowry

Folio 67b

sinodus, sayn [seine, net(?); *sinodus*, bream (fish); see fol. 173b]
arbosus, sayle
alluus, wombe [belly]
abissis, depnes
alnus, a neldyr [an alder (tree)]
cristallus, crystall
humus, þe grownde
bissus, whyte sylke
papirus, bulerusche
smaragdus, presyous stone
vannus, vanne [*OED*, *van*, sb.[2], winnowing basket or shovel]

colus, dystafe
facelus, lytyll bote [boat?]
porticus, porche
egiptus, egypt
diptongus, dyptong [diphthong; *OED* first cit., 1483]
vulgus, comynpepyll
pelagus, the see
vitus, venome

Folio 68a

lepus, a watt [*OED, wat,* hare]
thus, frankynsens
annus, old wyfe
tribus, kynred [kindred]
porticus, porche
manus, hond
idus, an edyll [a needle: also glossed *acus*; but there is confusion with (or a pun on) *idol*; *idus, idos,* species, form, shape]
pinus, pinetre

Folio 68b

specus, den
penus, spense [spence, cupboard]
dens, tothe
calx, hele
quadrans, fardyng [farthing]
torrens, ryuer
calebs, stele

Folio 69a

adeps, fatnes
infans, ynglyng [youngling]
parens, fadyr and modyr
princeps, prince
effrons, mad
forceps, tongis [*tongis* added above]
audax, bolde
pulex, a flee
vibex, a strype [blow with a whip; *vibex,* mark of a blow; see *vibex, wale,* below]
obex, bar [for a door]
supellex, couerlet
forfex, a seserys [scissors]
forpex, peyr of tongis
cortex, brak [bark (of a tree), metathesized]
silex, flynte
caryx, flag [*MED, flagge,* n. (1), reed or rush]
nux, nvtte
frutex, busch
dux, duke
coniunx, a man or hys wyfe

Folio 69b

fornix, a strumpetys howse [strumpet's house, bordello; *fornix,* furnace, a common euphemism; in Juvenal and Suetonius, brothel (lit. vault; brothels were situated in underground vaults) or one who gives oneself up to prostitution]
grex, flok
rex, kyng
calyx, chalis
fenix, fenuse [phoenix]
vibex, wale [weal, mark of a blow; this and the following gloss are interlinear, in a different hand]
forfex, shyris [shears]
Explicit Genera

Folio 70a–b

[English proverbs with Latin translations, edited by B. J. Whiting in J. B. Bessinger and R. P. Creed, eds., *Medieval and Linguistic Studies in Honor of Francis Peabody Magoun* (London, 1965), pp. 274–89. The British Library notice of material published from Add. MS 37075 incorrectly attributes the edition of the proverbs to J. W. Bartlett. Whiting's name is Bartlett Jere Whiting.]

Folio 84b

[Latin and English interlinear glosses; the latter are recorded.]
superus, rochet [smock, frock, cloak, or mantle]
iocus, a pley
infernus, hell
auernus, hell
vitellus, þe yolke of an egge
rastrum, rake
porrum, leke [leek]
pelagus, see
vulgus, comyn pepull
carbisus, seyle
sequium, gooldis [gold coins(?); *MED, gold,* 3. (d)]
supellex, couelert [error for *coverlet*]
balneum, bath
delicium, delyte
epulum, incite [not clear; ***epulum,*** banquet]
cepe, onyoun
zizannia, drawke or darnell [*MED, drauke,* a weed]
limus, slyme
lues, a spote [plague spot]
penum, spense [cupboard]
pus, fylth
mammona, myssegotyn good [misbegotten god [Mammon]; misgotten good(s)?]
macte[?] in vocatio, virtuose
frugis, profetabyll
arma, wepyns
mine, thretyngis [threats]
penates, privy goodis or chambyrs [*goodis,* gods]
diuicie, richesse

Folio 98a

[Continuation of Latin grammar, with synonyms and exemplary Latin verses following each Latin word. Only the key words in English are provided below, except when the Latin verses are of particular interest. The arrangement is roughly alphabetical.]
anima, sawlys
aula, hallys
auis, byrdys

Folio 98b

archas, chestys
arduus, heythys [heights]
avxilum, helpys
aqua, watres or flodes
argilla, clay
aenum, pannys or vessellis

Folio 99a

affecto, covet
auriga, carteris cartis [carters' carts] or waynys
aper, swyne
aries, shepe
astruit, graunt or affyrme

Folio 99b

[Illegible], graunt
[abdicat], deny
adiuuat, helpe
aufert, take awey
alloquitur, speke to
auget, hepe or gaddyr togyddyr
arcet, costreyn[e]
azinus, assys
accusans, accuse

Folio 100a

abiudicat, deme or to gyve be dome [judge or give by judgment]
autor, makeris
audax, hardymen
avidus, couetous men
alit, noryssh
albescit, wex whyte [*wex,* wax, turn]
amonium, [glossed at beginning of next leaf]

Folio 100b

oyntmentis
amurca, draggis [dregs]
augur, wycchys [witches; the Lat. verses equate witches and mathematicians]
anus, olde wyff[e] [A portion of the Latin verses: "Dum dormitat anus velut ancer sibilat anus." It demonstrates, comically, the two meanings of *anus* and may be translated "While the anus (old woman) sleeps, the anus hisses like a goose."]
arbor, treys
assis, halpeny
astucia, wysdam
agit, make an ende

Folio 101a

apothecas [not glossed]
pignoria, weddys [*OED*, *wed*, sb., pawn-pledges]
appellat, calle be name
aperit, opyn
audet, presumme or to char[?] [cropped; possibly error for *dare*(?)]
arat, ery [plow; error for *eryn*(?)]
alget, wex colde [*wex,* wax, turn]
ara, auter [altar]
amicit, cover or to hyde

Folio 101b

[Illegible], an hepe or a hy[ll] [probably glossing Lat. *agger*]
heremytis, recl[usis] or ancressys [probably glossing Lat. *anachoreta*]
ambulo, go
aue, hayle or to fare well
animussis, dowte
arcuo, to croke or to bowe
ala, batell
bellus, fayre or semely

Folio 102a

beatus, blyssyd or happy
bracte, breches [breechcloths, britches]
beuer, beuer or brokke [beaver or badger; the Lat. includes "sunt testicli castratos," the belief that beavers were killed for their testicles, or that they bit them off and tossed them to hunters to avoid being killed]
besancius, besauntis or gyftis [MED, *besaunt,* gold coin; 3. (e) by extension, especially in Biblical contexts, mental or spiritual gift]
boletus, muscheromys or paddystolys [*MED* and *OED* have *paddock stool* but not *paddy-*; Lat. includes "asperagus . . . quos fructus terre faciunt tonitrus pluuie que," the belief that asparagus and mushrooms were produced by thunder or rain]
balsamus, bamys [balms]

Folio 102b

bachus, wyne
[Illegible], bassys of howsys or sellis [bases of houses or floors; Lat. probably *basis*]
batulus, busschellis
barrus, elefaunt
balantes, shepe
baiulo, to bere
baltheus, gyrdyllys
betam, calstoke [*MED, calstok,* cabbage stalk, sometimes used as a suppository]
bilis, wreth or anger
bilibris, dowbyll bokys [two books bound together(?); Lat. includes *bifores,* double doors]

Folio 103a

boo as, to cry [*boo as, sic* as two words]
buccina, trumpys [trumpets]

bostar, herthmen [herdsmen; *bostar*, cattle shed]
boetes, lodesterre
bombex, selkworm

Folio 103b

[bufo], todis and froggis
blata, bakkis [bats]
brauium, the endlesgame [not in *OED*; error for *end of [the] game*? Lat.: "Mercedem cursus brauium victoria donat"; *Brauium* = *brabeum*, reward, prize]
bractea, thynne pecis [thin pieces, slices]
bruma, wynter
brucus, a bresis [error for *brese*, locust]
canis, howndis
celum, hevyn
catacumba, priveys [privies; Lat.: "est latrina locus idem catacumba cloaca / signat idem quia triste tegens tristega vocata," which includes the association of privies or sewers with melancholy]
corda, ropys or cordis

Folio 104a

canterus, cuppys [Eng. word is faint]
culter, knyvys
cophinus, panyers or lepys [baskets]
caseus, chesefatis or scoppys [cheese vats or scoops; *OED*, *scoop*, 3, cheesescoop (first cit., 1747)]
cinctoria, gyrdelys hosye or hokys [*MED*, *hok* no relevant entry]
camisia, shertis
crudelis, cruell; **improbus,** bowystus [crude, cruel]
chorus, cumpanyes and legiouns

Folio 104b

companye and legyouns [repeated at top of leaf]
campana, bellis
campus, feldis
cortine, curteynys or hallyngis [halling, piece of tapestry used as a hanging]
certamen, stryves or debatis
crinis, herys

Folio 105a

corona, crownys
currus, charys or cartys
cithera, harpys [Lat.: "Et delirare discordes inde fermitur / Deliro discordo delire demodico"; note alliteration and pun, *de* + *liro*]
dubitat, dow[te]
domus, howsys or dwellyngis

Folio 105b

[domina], lady, wymmen
doctor, maystyrs [corr. from *mass-*]
destruo, destroy
dumos, busshes or tufftis
diu[i]cie, rychesses
dapes, metis [meats, food]
equus, horsys

Folio 106a

enucos, geldydmen [*enucos*, error for *eu-*; Lat.: "Dicimus enuchos castratos siue spadones / Si que metrum ementulatus messet"]
estimo, trowe or leve [believe]
famulus, seruauntis
foramen, holys [holes]
fossa, dychys or dennys

Folio 106b

thevys [Lat. omitted; probably *fur*]
gladius, swerdis
graphium, poyntellis [pointel, stylus]
gratulor, to ioy
gibbus, botchys [swellings, tumors; Lat. distinguishes tumors in the chest and on the back (*struma*)]
horreo, to dred
ignis, fyr
ianua, gatis
insanus, woode [mad, insane]

Folio 107a

infernus, hellys
iunicus, rysshes [rushes]
incenso, sense [cense]
interimit, kylle
incantatrix, wycchys or wycche-crafte [Lat.: "Venificas magicas dicas lamas que sagas / Istis signantur eadem quibus associantur / Hec incantatrix stix sagana prestigiatrix / Histrio vel palpo mimus vel gesticulator," associating witches with actors]
ioculator, harlotis and glotonys [Lat.: "Est epulo nebulo paracitus scurra lecator / Sic pantomimus comedus vel ioculator / De serpente nepa dictos hijs adde nepotes," indicating more low opinion of actors]
lapis, stonys
lectus, beddys
luna, the mone

Folio 107b

bokys [Lat. omitted, probably *liber*, associated punningly with the next entry]
libellum, wastell [fine bread]
laynerys or garterys [Lat. omitted, probably *ligula*]
luto, mukke or dunge
mare, þe see
meretrix, strumpettis [Lat.: "Est meretrix scortum thays et lupa cap [?] chimera / Post nonam prestans nonaria mergitur illis," associating brothels and nunneries, as in *Hamlet*]
mappa, bordcloþis or towellys
miles, knyghtis
materia, materys of howsys or wallys

Folio 108a

manifestat, show[e] [or] to make opyne
morior, to dey [followed by 19 lines of Lat. synonyms]

Folio 108b

deth [also glosses *morior*, preceding leaf]
nauis, shyppys
nobil, nobill or dowthy

Folio 109a

nemus, wodys
narro, telle
negligit, dyspyse
olla, pottis [here the scribe initiates the practice of occasional interlinear glossing of some of the Latin synonyms]
amphora, tancarde; **lagena,** galon [subentry]
plumar, coverlet[is] [or] pelowy[s]
toral, bed styd; **tapitibus,** tappet[is] [subentry]
perichilides, ornamentis [Lat.: "Cum ceruicali ceruici dante calorem" *ceruici* gl. to þe neke)]
lunula, cressawnde; **fassia,** bond-[is]; **peplum,** wympyll; **armillas,** oychys; **monile,** oche; **crinale,** here stryng; **fibula,** bootun; **limbus,** heme; **fimbria,** heme; **ora,** heme; **tiara,** bonet [subentry; *cres-*

sawnde, *MED*, *cresaunt*, 2. (a), crescent-shaped ornament; *oychys*, *MED*, *nouch*, gem, brooch, etc.; *stryng*, not in *MED*]
pinguedo, fatnesse
sumen, suet [subentry]
prostibulum, a strumpettis howse, kyttchyne [Lat.: "Fornix prestibulum genethea crepedo lupanar / Vinum significat papina coquina culma," indicating *fornix* (furnace) as synonym for *bordello*]

Folio 109b

sanctus eligius, seynt loy
[pon]dus, bordonnys, pakkys, or fardellys
clitella, pake; **fascis,** fagote; **moles,** budeyne [subentry; *budeyne*, error for *bur-*]
[p]anes, breddis or daynty metis
artocapi, craknel; **pastelli,** pastey; **liba,** wastel; **placeta,** symnel; **artocrea,** pye; **artocaseus,** chese cake; **simila**, mele [subentry; *craknel*, *crakenel*, kind of bread; *symnel*, *simnel*, fine bread]
pallia, mantellys
matrix, martyr; **beuer,** beuer; **sirogrillus,** sqwerel [subentry; *martyr*, error for *martyn*; *sqwerel*, squirrel fur]
pellicium, pylchye, clothys, skynnys [*pylche*, pilch, garment made of skin dressed with hair]
puer, children
pericula maris, pere[llis] of the see
letophagus, [?]ory; **acceramnia**, owrarons; **escus**, þe gete of see; **silla**, scalow; **vortex**, whorllepyte [interlinear; *owrarons*, over irons; *acceramnia*, refers to a process of welding steel over iron, not in *MED*, *OED*; *gete of see*, jet, waterspout; *scalow*, Scylla (the scribe misunderstands) not in *OED*]

popina, kychennys
pellis, skynnys
pondus, weyghtis

Folio 110a

sanctus egidius, saynt gyle
priscus, olde
decrepitus, a crepyl; **velus**, old; **longeuus**, longlyuyd [subentry; *velus*, error for *vetus*]
piger, slought [sloth]
desuescat, ys not wonte [subentry]
pluuie, raynes or dewys
porto, to bere
pargo, to goo
rimor, enserche
rete, nettis
lina, nettis [of] flex or hempe; **retio**, cache; **allaquirare**, to loose [subentry]
rusticus, vplondysmen
rudit, bustis; **egrestis**, tyl mann [interlinear; *bustis*, *boistous*, crude, unmannerly; *tyl man*, *tillman*, plowman, peasant]

Folio 110b

vplondysmen [repeated]
epiliones, sheperdis; **hulio sive custos mulorum**, mulkeper; **buculcos**, keper of kyyne; **subulcos**, keper of swyne [subentry; *buculous*, altered from *subulcas*]
rotundum, rownde
effigio, lyknesse; **spera**, mapa mundi [subentry; Chaucer uses the Gallicized form of the word, *mappemounde*; the connection with *rownde* is evidently the oval shape of contemporary maps]
regredior, go agayne
sera, barrys or lokkis
scutum, sheldys or balerys [not in *MED*, *OED*, *b-* or *v-*]
sepulcrum, gravys

semita, pathis or stretis
computa, cownte; **callet**, to hearde [subentry; *hearde*, harden]

Folio 111a

sol, son[ne]
stultus, folys
inscius, not knoyng; **brutus**, dounce; **idiota**, ydyet [subentry]
scannum, setys [seats]
seres, cornys
seminum, sede, tymys of sowyng
seminum, sede; **sero**, sow; **sementura**, natura semens [subentry; glossed in Lat.]
scutella, platerys or dysshys
socius, felowys
signifer, baner bereris
signifer, tokyn berer; **p[?]ssarius**, tapyr berer; **vexillifer**, banerer, banner berer [subentry]

Folio 111b

[Illegible], berer
[splendet], shynne [shine]
spurcitia, ffelthe
scabiosus, scaby, scabbys, or botchys
glabrio, scale; **glabriosus**,scalde; **scabies**, scale; **scabiosus**, scale; **pustula**, puscheboche; **ulcus**, boche [subentry; *puscheboche*, not in *OED*; first cit. for *pus*, 1541]
serpens, serpentis
ydrus, watyradyr; **ydra**, water adyr; **scorpio vel scorpius**, scorpion
sacrifico, kylle or to sacrifyce
lamo, to tere; **lanistas**, bocher [subentry; *bocher*, butcher]
soclaris, shone or cordewayne
calceus, shoo; **pero**, pynsoun; **aluta**, cordweyne; **aluta**, corweyne [subentry; *pynsoun*, *OED*, *pinson*,[2] thin shoe; slipper or pump]
telum, darthys or arowys
hastile, shafe; **catapulta**, brode arow; **missile**, datte; **arundo**, rede; **gesas**, gleve [subentry; *shafe*, error for *-te*; *datte*, error for *dar-*; *rede*, reed; *gleve*, *MED*, *glaive*, lance, spear]
terra, erthe
ops, dea terre; **rea**, dea terre [subentry; *dea terre*, glossed in Lat.]

Folio 112a

thalamus, t[entis] [evidently an error; see *tentoria* below; perhaps *t(resorhows)*]
conclaue, privy chambyr; **canopea**, canope; **penates**, privy chambyr; **reticulum**, nett; **canopeum**, canape [subentry]
te[m]pla, templys, cherchys
monasteria, monastere; **delubra**, cherche; **fane**, cherche
tentoria, tentis
canopea, canope; **tentoria**, a tente; **papiliones**, pavylyoun; **canope castro**, de illo castell; **conum**, crest [subentry; *de illo castell*, glossed in Lat.]
turribulum, vessellys of ensence [*vessellys*, altered from *w-*]
acerra, senser [subentry]
ventus, wyndis
flame, blast; **aura**, wynde; **fonsolanus**, soþe este wynd; **vultnus**, norþe este wynd; **eurilo**, est; **eoy**, of þeste; **chromus**, þe norþe west; **zepherus**, þe soþe west wynde; **chorus**, wynde; **archo**, id est a polo archico [subentry; *of þeste*, *of the east*; *id est...archico*, glossed in Lat.]
vinum, wynes
merum, wyne; **bacus**, id est deus; **liber**, id est deus; **ydromel, mulsum**, swette wyne; **sisera**, bere or ale; **pigmentum**, pyment; **mustum**, muste; **melliccum**, hosey;

falernum, wyne; **sapa**, wyne [interlinear; *id est deus*, glossed in Lat.; *pyment*, wine mixed with honey and spices; *hosey*, error for *honey*]
vestis, clothys
eximias, a doyng ofe [subentry; *a doyng ofe*, doing off, removing (clothing)]

Folio 112b

vinea, vines
vinetum, wyne yerd; **vua**, grape; **propago**, wyn [subentry; *wyn*, word following is deleted; *propago* refers to vineculture by grafting]
venter, belyes
aluiolus, trewyth [subentry; *trewyth*, error for *trowyth* (*trough*)]
Explicit
[Etymologies (some fanciful) with a few English glosses follow.]

Folio 113b

vitricus, step fadyr; **a vitrum quasi vitrius custos**, brekyll [*MED*, *brekil*, 2., as a noun, fragment of food; the stepfather is the keeper of broken meats] **signifer**, tokyne berer
[A series of homographs or homophones, e.g., *Cecula C scripta serpens fertur fore C ceca. Secula scripta per S sunt tempora longa vel etas*.]

Folio 120a

cecula, slowe worme
Non tendit peritum qui vult audire peritum, a wyse man

Folio 121a

pendere, behangyd

Folio 122b

oriens, este; weste, **occidens**; northe, **borias**; sowthe, **haustri**

Folio 123a

licet, ys set by
licet, prese
serta, potte
seras, sildom
serum, slow

Folio 123b

prohedmo, sugerne [sojourn]
diutus, tary
lego, sende
lego, rede
colo, make feyre
linitis, to dawbe
linitis, a noynt
lini, flexe [flax]

Folio 124b

[Some glosses illegible]
cuperum, coper
ferrum, yrne
calibs, stele
electrum, peuter
stannum, tynne
plumbum, lede
desauri, latynne [latten, an alloy like brass]
mala, cheke
malum, apyll
malus, maste
stringimus, bende
cesaries, here [hair]

Folio 125a

comeso, ete
comefacio, etyn
irundo, vatyr leche [water leech]
propago, branche
propago, kynrede

Folio 125b

lustri, clennes [cleanness]
dulcor, swetnes

Folio 126a

boreas, norþe wynd [repeated]
auster, sowth wynde, vynde
eurus, northen
affricus, sowth west
zepherus, sowth west
eurus, west north west
aquilo, north north west

Folio 127a

[Exercises in the conjugations]
domo, to tame
do, to yeve
domo, to tame
mico, schyne
iuuo, helpe
sto, stonde
plico, to folde
frico, rubbe
sono, to sownde
neco, sle [slay]
veto, warne
lauo, wasche
ceco, to kutt
cubo, to lye
tono, to sownde
nexo, knytt

Folio 127b

replico, folde aȝene
supplico, beseche
circundo, cumpas a bowte [repeated on this folio as *compasse a bowte*]
pessundo, trede vndyr the fote
venundo, selle
satisdo, geve i nowe
reddo, to ȝelde
facit mictum, to pisse

Folio 128a

facit micam, to schyne
asto, to stounde [astound, astonish]
obsto, with stonde [repeated on this folio]
consto, to cost or to be
accommodare, lende
aunstare, stond a fore [*aunstare,* error for *ante-*?]
donare, to yeve [repeated on this folio as *ȝeve*]
precellere, passe
preualere, preuayle
statuere, ordeyne, to yeve an offesse
exhibere, fynde
facere vtile, make profitable
corrigere, mende
panere, synge a fore [*panere,* error for *pandere*?]
nutrire, nurysche

Folio 128b

concubo, to lye
crepo, breke or to sownde
lauo, wasche

Folio 129a

lauo, wasche [repeated, as are several other items on this folio]
poto, drynke
crepo, breke
frico, rubbe
plico, folde
mico, schyne
frico, rubbe
plico, folde
mico, schyne
neco, strike, sle
cubo, lye
crepo, breke
seco, kutt
sono, sownde
veto, warne
dimico, to fyȝthe [fight]

Folio 130a

mordeo, byȝthe
cedo, bete
cado, falle
curro, to ren
tondeo, to schere
fallo, begyle
spondeo, to be hote [promise]
tundo, knokke
cano, synge
pello, putt away
posco, aske
pario, bryng forthe
do, ȝeve
sto, stonde
tango, towche
pango, make a counawnte [*make,* altered from *fur-*; *counawnte,* covenant]
tendo, streche owte
tollo, take away
pungo, to prykke
pedo, to farte [Lat. reads in part "Pedo simul disco" ("I fart and simultaneously learn")]
disco, lerne
parco, spare
pendo, honge
remordeo, byte a geyne
posco, aske
sto, stonde
do, geve
disco, lerne

Folio 130b

nideo, to stynke
mordeo, to byte
gaudeo, to ioye
yrgeo, constreyne
indulgeo, to ȝeve hede [*MED, hed,* n. (1) (= head), no phrase *yeven hed,* but 5. a. (a) *haven hed of,* rule or control; *hed,* n. (2) (= heed), 2. (a) *yeven hed to,* take pains with]
augeo, encrese
langueo, wayle
vigeo, thryve
frigo, to fryy

Folio 131a

algeo [gloss illegible]
frigo, to frye
langueo, to morne
ameo, to desyre
fleo, to wepe
oleo, to stynke
redoleo, smell swete
redoleo, stynke

Folio 131b

vileo, to be fowle
valeo, to may [*MED, mouen,* v. (3), 1. (a) be strong, prevail; be worthy]
soleo, to be wonte
timeo, to drede
moneo, warne
neo, spynne
teneo, holde
maneo, dwelle
permaneo, to a byde
torqueo, to be slowe [slain; altered from *torment*]

Folio 132a

torreo, to make a ferde
careo, lakke
torreo, toste [toast; Lat. ppl. *tostum,* distinguished from *torritum,* ppl. of *torreo* above]
hereo, to cleue to
mereo, to sorowe
mereor, deserue
censeo, calle or to numbyr
niteo, schyne
lateo, lye prevy [lie in hiding]

Folio 132b

pasco, to fede
caueo, to be warre
faueo, to fauor
sero, sow
lauo, wasche
soluo, paye
voluo, wrappe
cognosco, knowe
amicio, chothe [error for *cl-*]
sepelio, bury
singulcio, to snobbe [*OED*, v.[1], sob]
venio, to be solde
forneo, to be hote
conniueo, twynkyll with the ye [wink]
ferueo, covett
liueo, do lechery
seueo, be cruell
paueo, drede
maneo, dwelle
luceo, schyne
polluceo, schyne [*polluceo*, error for *pel-*]
mulceo, swage [assuage, soothe]

Folio 133a

sorbeo, sowpe [soak (bread, etc.) in liquid]
censeo, calle
misceo, mengylle [mingle, mix]
soluo, to pay
vomo, cast owte
fundo, schede
vinco, ouercom

Folio 133b

rego, gouerne
lego, rede
bibo, drynke
scribo, wryte
vello, plukke
rumpo, breke
parco, spare
emo, bye
linquo, forsake
verto, turne
scribo, wryte
bibo, drynke
discumbo, sytt att mete
dico, say
vinco, ouercom
cresco, growe
compesco, constrayne
dispesco, departe [divide, share]
disco, lerne
posco, aske

Folio 134a

ico, smyte
glisco, couett
conquinesco, bekke with the hede [nod]
vinco, ouyrcom
dico, sey
disco, lerne
compesco, constreyne
posco, aske

Folio 134b

ludo, pley
cedo, goo a waye
cudo, smyte
strido, gnasche
sido, sytt
pedo, to fart [Lat.: "Nullum fido gerit quo turpe sonat fit in edi" ("Anyone who makes a bad sound while eating generates no confidence"); this belief seems to be the contrary of Martial 10.14.9-10]
reddo, ȝelde aȝene
prendo, take
plaudis, to ioy
claudo, schytt [shut]
fundo, schede
findo, cleve [cleave, split]
pindo, bake
cado, falle

tundo, knokke
rudo, cry as an asse

Folio 135a

commedo, ete
diuisi, departe [divide, share]
mando, ete
reddo, ȝelde
findo, cleue [cleave, split]
fundo, putt owte
pando, schewe

Folio 135b

prendo, take
prehendo, take
tundo, knokke
contundo, knocke to gedyr
incido, fall in
occido, slyde
recido, falle agayne
condo, make
pando, schewe

Folio 136a

tendo, streche
intendo, tak hede
precido, kutt a fore
recido, goo away
excedo, passe
concedo, grawnte
precedo, go a fore
mergo, drowne

Folio 136b

surgo, to a ryse
vngo, to a noynte
pungo, to pryke
pango, make a counawnte
lego, rede
tango, towche
ago, to doo
frango, breke
pango, make a counawnte [repeated; see above]
tango, to towyche
ago, to doo
frango, breke
dego, lyue
ambigo, dowte
satago, dowte
satago, enforse

Folio 137a

sugo, soke [suck]
mergo, drowne
frigo, frye
pungo, to prykke
clanctum, to trumpe [sound a trumpet]
cinctum, gyrde
auctum, constreyne
tinctum, to dye
planctum, to wayle

Folio 137b

intellego, vndyrstonde
diligo, love
necligo, dispyse
eligo, chese [choose]
perlego, to rede ofte
religo, to rede a ȝen
extingo, quenche
traho, drawe
alo, norysche
vello, plukke
alo, norysche
molo, grynde
tollo, lyfte vpp
cello, passe

Folio 138a

percello, smyte
sallio, to salte
salio, skyppe
psallo, synge [sing]
facio, make
icio, smyte

inficio, make
occido, slyde
ambigo, dowte

Folio 138b

benefacio, do well
perficio, make perfytt
dic, sey
duc, lede
fac, make [altered from *l*-; scribe started to write *lede* again]
fer, bere
fodio, dygge
fugio, to flee
rapio, ravesche
capio, take
sapio, to saver
quero, to seche [beseech]
peto, aske
sapio, to savyr
cupio, couett
tero, breke
lacessitum [glossed on next leaf]

Folio 139a

to desyre to tere
visitum, desyre to see
capessi[tum], desyre [to take]
facessitum, desyre to make
pinso, bake
inquiro, seye
pario, bryng forthe
appareo, opyn
reperio, fynde
comperio, knowe
aperio, opyn
experior, knowe
operior, tary

Folio 139b

quatio, breke
vomo, caste [vomit]
primo, thurste downe [*thurste,* thrust]
emo, bye
demo, to do a waye
cano, synge [sing]
gigno, begett
pono, putt
contempno, dyspyse
lino, to dawbe
pono, putt
succino, synge [sing]

Folio 140a

contem[pno], dispyse
lino, to dawbe
strepo, make a noyse
clepo, to stele
scalpo, to clawe
carpo, to tose wolle [*tose,* toze, card]
repo, to crepe
lingo, to lykke
delinquo, trespas
coquo, to sethe

Folio 140b

accelero, to haste or to hyy [added at top of leaf in later hand]
tero, breke
gero, bere
curro, runne
verro, to wrote [root, as swine]
vro, to brenne
quero, to seke
sero, to plant or to lokke
verto, to torne
vergo, torne
lacesso, to desyre to tere
viso, desyre to see

Folio 141a

capesso, desyre to take
facesso, desyre to make
pinso, bake
casinatisso, chap or to chyne [Added twice in later hand; *MED, chine,* v. (1) to crack or split; *chined,* chapped]

pecto, to kembe [comb]
necto, to knytt
plecto, punysche
sterto, rowte [added twice in later hand; snore]

Folio 141b

firmare, make stedfast
representare, to present
statuere, ordeyne
retinere, with holde
manere, byde [bide, wait]
acuo, make sherpe
arguo, repreve [reprove]
ruo, falle
luo, punysche
pluo, to rayne
struo, to enforme [put in proper form or order]
fluo, flowe

Folio 142a

solui, paye
ferueo, to be hote
frendeo vel frendo, gnasche
tergeo vel tergo, wype
conniueo vel conniuo, twynkyll with the ye [wink]
fulgeo vel fulgo, schyne
video vel vido, see
sorbeo vel sorbo, to sope [sop, soak (bread etc.) in liquid]
oleo vel olo, to stynke
censeo vel censo, call
excelleo vel excello, passe
caueo vel cauo, to be ware
sedeo vel sedo, sytt
coaleo vel coalo, growe
nexo, knytt
texo, weve

Folio 142b

aperio, to opyn
eo, to goo
haurio, drawe [pull]
reperio, fynde
cambio, change
vincio, bynde
venio, come
audio, to here
auibio, covett [*auibio,* error for *-dio*?]
vincio, bynde
vercio, to ameve [make a movement]
nescio, to knowe [error for *not to know*]
sencio, to fele
saliio, lepe
sepio, to hegge [hedge, make hedges]

Folio 143a

pario, bryng forthe
farcio, to stuffe
haurio, drawe
sepio, to hegge
reuenio, com ageyne
repertum, fynde
audio, to here
salio, skyppe
venio [glossed on next leaf]

Folio 143b

to be solde
sepelio, bery
amicio, clothe
adeo, go to
audio, here
lino, dawbe
tero, breke
sino, know
Explicit

Folio 144a

[Treatise on deponent verbs, glossed interlinearly, with rhymed Latin couplets.]
auguror, devyne [practice divination]
auxilior, helpe
ampullor, boste [boast]

apiscor, gete [get]
adulor, glose [flatter]
aucupor, to fowle [go fowling, catch birds]
ariolor, devyne [practice divination; *ariolor* = *hariolor,* prophesy, divine]
aruspicor, idem [glosses the preceding]
apocalipsor, shewe
auspicor, devyne [practice divination]
aspernor, dyspyce
antestor, idem testare [*idem,* error for i.e.]
aristor, gaddyr erys [gather ears (of grain)]
amicor, be a frende
arbitror, deme [judge]
auertor, dyspyce
auersor, curse
auxionari, do huckestry [*MED, huksterie,* retail trade, peddling; only one cit., from *Piers Plowman*]
argumentor, argew
architector, i.e. edificare
accidiari, be slowe
anxior, be grewous [full of grief]
ancillor, serue
altercor, stryve [fight]
aquor, watyr
ancillor, serue
adulteror, i.e. luxuriare [beginning with this entry, the scribe is reluctant to gloss taboo words, which he nonetheless includes]
blandior, glose [flatter]
bacor, woode [mad (insane), i.e., to run mad]
carnificor, to slee
contor, serche
calumnior, repreve [reprove]
calipsor, i.e. velare, to couer
concionor, speke to [*concionor,* altered from *concio,* false start in Lat.]
conor, enforce
cuntor, tari [tarry]
crissor, luxuare [error for *luxuriare*: *crissor,* move the haunches, like a dog wagging its tail; hence, wanton, licentious behavior]
commistor, grynde

Folio 144b

complector, klype [embrace]
causor, plette [plead, in law]
commentor, expowne [expound (upon)]
crassor, make fatte
comminor, to threte
comitor, folow
conuertor, turne [added at bottom of leaf, with mark indicating where it belongs in text]
carminior, charme [sing, chant a charm]
cachinnor, make mowes [*MED, moue,* n. (2); *maken moues,* laugh, ridicule]
conspicor, to gader erys [gather ears (of corn)]
conspicor, loke downe [*conspicor* repeated, perhaps in error]
cauillor, i.e. decipere
conuicior, repreve [reprove]
detestor, curse
dignor, wothsafe [vouchsafe]
delector, delyte
cumdominari, haue lordshyp
despicor, loke downe
despicor, gader erys
emulo, folow, to long [long for]
enitor, enforse
episcopor, be a byshop
epulari, ete
expergistor, wake [awaken, trans. verb]
execror, curse
eiulor, wepe
fabulor, talke
famulor, serue
fateor, knowleg [acknowledge]
frustror, desseve
furor, stele

for, speke
feueror, do vsery
fruticor, growe
fungor, vse
fruor, idem [glosses preceding entry]
fatiscor, fayle [*fayle* altered from illegible false start]
frumentor, gader whete
fabricor, make

Folio 145a

gratulor, thanke
gradior, to goo
grassor, contravadere
grecor, folow grekis
grator, thanke
glorior, to yoye [joy, rejoice]
gesticulor, to yoye
gratior, thank
regracior, to thank ye
hospitor, to harbur
histrionor, to yogyll [juggle; indicative of low esteem of actors]
hospitor, to herbur or to be herberd [*hospitor,* repeated]
iantor, dyne
iocundor, be mery
iuntor, folow
iaculor, cast
iurgor, chyd
iocor, pley
insidior, espye
imaginor, ymage [*MED, imaginen,* imagine]
inficiari, deme
irastor, be wrothe
ioculor, yogell [juggle]
labor, slyde
lamentor, sorow
lacrimor, wepe
letor, be glad
leniscor, do a way
licior, prese [appraise]
licitor, idem [also glosses *prese*]
liquor, folow [error for *flow*]
loquor, speke
lucror, wynne *vel* gette [obtain (money)]

Folio 145b

lecor, luxuriare [scribe is reluctant to provide English gloss]
lenocinor, idem est [*lenocinor, leno,* pimp]
luctor, wrastyll
limphor, to watyr
machinor, [?]are malum
medcor, do medicin
medicor, idem est
meditor, thenke
mecor, id est luxuriare [see *lecor* above]
mecor, [gloss illegible]
metor, mete [measure]
mereor, deserue
morior, dy
mercor, marchandyse
miniculor, help
minor, threte
metrior, mete [measure]
meretricor, id est luxuriare [see *lecor* above]
molior, to ymage [see *imaginor* above]
miror, to merwell [marvel]
miseror, mercy
miserere, idem est
malignor, curse
metuor, drede
memoror, mynd
moderor, mesure [(to) moderate; *moderor,* altered from *modo-*]
meridionari, ete at mydday
nansciscor, purchesse
nascor, spryng [originate]
naufrangor, perische in a shipe
nemor, uaneloqui
nugor, to yape [jape, speak nonsense]
nutor, wake
nitor, enforse
negocior, do marchandise

marcari, idem est
perhibit, is seyd
ominor, to dyvyne
operior, abyde
obliuiscor, to for gete
opinor, deme
ordior, speak
opitulor, helpe
obstetricor, be a wydwyfe
operari, worke
ocior, be ydull
orior, spryng [originate]
pabulor, fede
pacior, suffyr
pocior, to vse
precor, pray
peculari, id est luxvriare [see *lecor* above; *peculari*, altered from *populari*]

Folio 146a

policeor, to be hote [offer, promise]
pedor, rube [not clear; *pedor*, break wind]
peregrinor, onpilgrymage
patorcinari, gape
prescolor, byde
periclitor, to perych or caperne, tampur [not clear; *periclitor*, test, put in danger]
propiciari, haue mercy
principor, be a prynce
precor, to wowe [woo, petition]
prolior, to battell
paciscor, make a cou[nawnte] [covenant]
perior, id est sapere
parcior, to parte
proficiscor, to goo
pigritor, be slowe
piscor, to fysch
populor, dystroy
questionor, aske a question
queror, playne [complain]
quietor, reste
rimor, enserche
rixor, chyde
ruspor, skrape
reor, trow
reminiscor, remembyr
reuertor, turne
reuersor, idem est
racionor, to resoun
ructor, to bulke [*MED, bolken*, belch; see fol. 331b]
suffragor, helpe
stupror, id est luxuriare [see *lecor* above]
sequor, folow
sector, idem
scititor, aske
scitor, idem est
solor, comfort
spacior, walke
scurror, to do harlattry [roguishness; but the word was assuming sexual meanings.]
stipulor, aske
speculor, to be holde
suscipicor, to haue in suspecyoun [*suscipicor*, altered to *suscp-*, but the corr. is deleted]
scrupulari, dowte

Folio 146b

sermocinor, sermonem factum [not glossed]
scortor, meretricor [see *lecor* above]
socior, caste lotte
stomachari, to be wexyde [vexed; not clear]
transalpinor, trans alpes
tergiuersor, to dyseyue
testor, wyttnesse
testificor, wyttnesse [altered from illegible false start]
tuor, be holde
tueor, defende
tutor, idem est
vlciscor, to wenge [avenge]
vagor, wandyr
vtor, vse

vereor, to drede
vescor, to ette
vaticinor, profycy
venor, hunte
verbosor, iangyll [jangle, chatter; *verbosor*, perhaps altered to *verbe-*]
verecundor, to wax a shamyd
varicor, to croke [*MED*, *croken*, 3, bow or stoop]
versificor, versevy [versify]
Sic deponentum minus perfectus habetur.
[These deponents lack the perfect tense]
largior, graunt or to be [something omitted; perhaps *be grawnted*]
experior, to saye [essay, try]
venerior, worchyp
meror, tary
osculor, kyse
ortor, monych [admonish; *ortor*, *hortor*]
criminor, blame
amplector, to klype [embrace]
scipulor, aske [*scipulor*, perhaps *st-*]
interpretor, expownde
hospitor, harbyr
Explicit liber deponentum
[End of the book of deponent verbs]

Folio 147b

[Latin glosses of Latin text; a few in English]
supinus, proyde [not clear]
falleris, hernesis [harnesses, armor]
hypogeum, treserhous [treasure-house; *hypogeum*, underground]
tardus, slow
sicophantes, pykfygis [not *in OED*; *sicophantes*, sycophants; cf. *pick-thanks*; orig. Gk. *sykophantes*, "fig-informers," those who informed on the illegal shipment of figs from Attica; *OED*, *pickthank*, sees no etymological relationship.]
styx, hel
rotabunt, hurle
terga, bakis of harte [clear, but sense obscure; *terga*=backs]
dilate, browt
elixa, [?]ode
precerere, barones
thoral, coverlite
stola, robe
cironomon, keruer [Lat.: "Cironomen mensis, lectis assistit aliptes" (glossed above *medicus*), "the carver helps at table, the doctor at bedside"]
eburnea, yvery [glossed in margin]
dumetis, busshiplace
latet, lurkyth [altered from *la-*]
pusio, chyld
revmaticus, snobby [*OED*, *snob*, v.[1], to sob; no entry for *snobby*; the Lat. suggests the sense *rheumy*]
pullus, fole [foal]
lappatus, raggyt [ragged]
hircus, goyth [goat]

Folio 148a

hynnulus, fawne
heredi, to a heyr [heir; *heredi*, altered from *th-*]
elephas, elefaunt
barrit, noyse [elephant's cry; *barrit*, *barritus*, elephant's cry]
honocoulus, bitterware [not in *MED*, *OED*, *honocoulus*, *onochiles*, bugloss, ox tongue]
bumbit, cryth [cryeth]
onager, wyld asse
rudit, cryt [cryeth]
rannuculus, lytyl frog
coaxat, crockyt [croaketh]
abra, bowyrmayd [*MED*, *bourmaid*, chambermaid; *abra*, handmaid]
macherus, mastyr kooke
heo, lorde [*heo*, altered from *eo*]
preparat, dytyt [dighteth, adorns]
stipes, stokis
andena, andyr[un] [andiron]
sustentus, borne vpe

deperit, spyllyth [perishes, dies]
duli, false
herilis, lordis
duliam, fa[l]se seruyse
promittit, be hotyt [promises]
placituram, to plese
pseudulus, fals
fecula, lyd [error for *lyght*? *fecula*, *fercula*, torch]
acinum, pypyn [*OED*, *pippin*, 1., pip, grape stone; *acinum*, berry]
caupo, tauerner

Folio 148b

musti, must
bibiones, flyys
premit, shewyt [showeth]
pigmeos, drewy[s] [*MED*, *dwergh*, dwarf; includes sp. *dreu*]
athocopis, symnel [*simnel*, bread made with fine flour]
anaphoi, cupe [*anaphoi*, *anaphus*, cup]
capsam, ston [*capsam*, *capsa*, box]
ydria, pote
amphora, tankard
eusebius, holy [*eusebius*, pious]
Explicit

Folio 149a

[Glosses of Latin verses]
gustus, a tastyng
augeo, encrese
fauor, fawyr
splendor, schynyng
flatus, blast
aier, aiyr
capitale columone, hede of a pelar
stibium, starche [Lat.: "in qua mulieres lauant facies" ("in which women wash their faces"); actually *stibium* = eye black]
calamistrum, starchyng yrun [Lat.: "cum quo crispantur crines" ("with which they curl their hair")]
sibula, an all [awl; *sibula*, error for *f*-]
stimulus, a nedylle
pugio draconis, styngyng of an addyr
palea, schaffe [chaff]
prima ordinacio belli, fore frunte of the batell

Folio 149b

acucior pars cultelli, egge of a knyffe
visus ocelli, syȝthe of the ye
incomitus, vntame
sevus, cruel
velox, swyfte
acerbus, sowyr [sour]
phalanx, wynge of batell
acella, arme pytt
ala . . . pars volucris, wynge
sublimis, hye
bonus, gode
subtilis, sotyll
profundus, depe
nutritus, nurysshyd
veho, carr[y]

Folio 150a

exeuntates vinearis, branchys of wynys [vines]
prestantes, branches stondyng owte
litera, letter
titulus, tetyll
altitudo, heythe
corona, crowne
conueniens, accordyng
aptatus, schapyd
adeptus, igeteyne [*MED*, *geten*, 8. (a), produce, create, accomplish (an errand); none of these meanings is satisfactory, though the word appears to be the past participle of *geten*]
attero, trede or to defowle [*attero*, rub off, weaken, destroy]
cimitorium, a chyrche ȝarde

obscurus, derke
aries, a ramme
aries, signum firmamenti, a sterre
aries . . . machina belli, an engyne of bateylle, a sowe [*OED, sow,* sb., 4., military engine with roof to cover advancing soldiers]

Folio 150b

antimo, suppose [added interlinearly in different hand; *antimo,* error for *animadverto,* or *intimo?*]
dico, sey
consumo, waste
feri, smyte
audio, here
absorbeo, sowpe
extraho, drawe owte
bibo, drynke
accipio, take ȝeftis
deripio, rawesche [ravish]
audio, here
macto, sle in sacrifice
acuo . . . significat actionem, to sharpe
aceo . . . significat passionem, to be sharpe
delinquo, to trespas
laxo, to slake [slacken]
hemnas, þe reynys of a brydyll
punire, punysche

Folio 151a

curam rependere, kepe or to take charge
cupio, cowett [covet]
fugo, dryve
transio, passe
causor, plete [plead, in court]
confirmo, helpe
ambio, go a bowte
circuctus, a compassyng a bowte
nota, a note [altered from *kn-*]

Folio 151b

arconius, a ryke of hey [rick of hay]
volta, a wovte [vault]
sinus, the crokyng of watyr [crooking, bight or bend]
iris, a reyne bowe
ille qui tenet arcum, an archar
architenens, keper of a contre [country]
articulus, breue membrum, a lytyll too
pressura, grewance [grievance]
digiti sunt proprier diuisiones manuum, of the hondis
articuli sunt pedum, of the fete

Folio 152a

reprehendere, repreve or to vndyr myne
coniunctus, ioynyd
sonorus, sownde full
cremo, burme [error for *burne*]
splendeo, schyne
cerno, deme or to be holde
assimilare, be lykynnyd [likened, compared]
ardea . . . auis, a herun
asiduus . . . studiosus, besy
as, a halpeny
assideo, be besy

Folio 152b

vendico, chalange
lauri vel edere, the bays of a lorell tre or of an yve tre [*edere, hedera*]
sacerdos id est sacerdotissa bachi, hoc est dei vini, god of wynys

Folio 153a

bubo . . . auis, an owyll
morbus, bubo sub ano, boche [botch, swelling]

buccula, parua gemma in galea, a stone in a helme
parua bucca, a lytyll cheke
pars zone pluris id est nobilis zone, the bokyll of a nobyll gyrdyll [*bokyll*, buckle; perhaps also glosses *buccula*]
bulla . . . tumor aquaris, a borbyll of watyr [*borbyll, bubble*; this sp. not in *MED*]
nola, cogbelle [*MED, coke-belle*, small bell]
vxor cauponis, tauyrnerys wyfe
taberna, tawerne
peruisus, wele awysyd [well advised]
firmus, stedefast or sekyr

Folio 153b

cauterium . . . signatum illo ferro, a make or a sporte [*cauterium*, branding iron; *MED* has no appropriate entry for *make*, nor does *OED* for *sporte*; Lat.: Hoc cauterium equivoce ad ij, id est instrumentum ferreum quo latrones solebant signari et iam solem animalia signari et est illud quo linquitur et [?] id est signatum illo ferro autore (refers to a thief's mark or brand, a branding iron, and an author's seal)]
cauea . . . scrobs, dysche [error for *dyche*]
casa, a cote [*cot*, cottage]
ara, swynys stye [*ara, hara]*
calix, pece or a chalys [*pece, OED, pece*, cup]
calix, nota vel passio mortis, a tokyn of dethe or a penance of dethe
calx . . . talus, an hele, a lyme stone
calculus, carbo, a ded cole
calculus, pondus, a charge [weight, load]
calculus, lapillus, a lytyl ston[e]

Folio 154a

dureo, make harde
callus, the hardenysse of the hele
callidus, a slyman
duricies manuum vel ped[um], hardnysse of the fette
duricies colli bouum, þe hardnysse of a nox neke [ox neck]
canis . . . piscis marinus, a sehou[nd]
canis . . . sidus celeste, a sterre of þe fyrmament
cancer, a crabbe, a cankyll [*MED* records this sp. for *canker*]
cacumen, hynesse
capella, capra, a gote, a chapell, a sterre [Lat.: vsus modernus confundet hanc differentiam et vtitur iam hic cancer, -cri, tam pro morbo quam pro pisse et signo (modern usage confuses the difference and uses *cancer, -cri*, for the illness as well as for the fish and the sign); Lat. also includes the name of a philosopher, "marciani" (= Martianus Capella)]

Folio 154b

carbunculus, a glouueryng teke, a carbunkyllstone, a felon [*glouueryng teke*, glowing tick (?) *MED, glouere*, probably the European glowworm; see fol. 315b, where the scribe does not gloss *nocteluca*, perhaps because he does not know the English word; *felon, MED, feloun*, carbuncle, abscess]
carchesium, the heythe of the maste [*carchesium*, Lat. explains that it also means incense boat]
cardo, a threscholde, a thystill [*cardo*, Lat. distinguishes *cardo, -uus*, and *cardo, -onis*]
cantor, synger
carmina, wychcr[af]te or prophesy [prophecy]

casus . . . lapsus, a slydyng
casus . . . euentus, a chawnce or an happe
cado, falle

Folio 155a

cassis, an helme
catula, lytyll whelpe
cathena, cheyne
cena, mete, a soper [Lat. distinguishes *cena* and *s[c]ena*]
ciclas, an yle of the see
coclea . . . scala, the vyse of a towre [*OED*, *vice*, sb.², winding staircase; *coclea*, snail]
coclea . . . testa, the schel of a fysche or off a snayle
cocliar, a spone [spoon]
columbar . . . vinculum vel iugum colli, the bonde of the nekke [Lat. also explains *columbar* as the hole through which the oar of a ship passes]

Folio 155b

concha, a schelfysche, a techel of the fysche [*techel*, error for *cochel*, cockle?]
chorus, busche[l]
chorea, a dawnce
cornuus . . . arbor, an hepe tre [*MED*, *hepe tre*, dog-rose tree or bush]
cornu, the hornes of a best, the for fronte of a batell
crudelis, cruel or spytuose
nouus, newe [subentry]
incoctus, rawe [subentry]

Folio 156a

cuna . . . cunabula, cradylle
curriculus, lytyll chare
cauo, to bore
fallo, begyle
cano . . . laudo, preyse
vaticinor, to profecye [subentry]
cancello, to with drawe letterys

Folio 156b

cedo . . . locum dare, to ȝeue place
carpo . . . decerper lanam, to tose [*OED*, *toze*, to card (wool)]
accuso, accuse [subentry]
reprehendo, repreve, reprove [subentry]

Folio 157a

sorbeo, to sowpe [sop, absorb]
cloaco . . . latrina, a privy [associated with *sorbeo* because it "sorbet feces"]
inclino, to bowe
inde diriuatur hic cliens, a servant [subentry]
dependencia montis, the haggyngis of a hyll [*haggyngis*, error for *hangyngis* (?); *MED* has nothing appropriate s.v. *honging* or *haggen*, to cut]
calculo, to a cownte
crepo, pinge [*OED*, *ping(e)*, has no appropriate sense; *crepo*, tinkle or fart]
decipere, to disseyve in wordis
circumbo, to goo a bowte
aduno, to make onne [to make one, unite]
colo . . . aro, to ere [plow; altered from *here*]

Folio 157b

colit formam, id est ornat, format, a raythe [arrayeth]
commendo . . . mandare in tutel[a], take to kepe [take into (one's) care]
facio, make
compono . . . sedo, to swage [assuage]

sepelio . . . facio, make
ordino . . . orno . . . simulo, to lykynne [liken, compare]
comparo . . . assimilare . . . emo, to by [buy]
condo . . . construere . . . facere, make or ordey[ne]
abscondo, hyde
condio . . . dulcorare, make savery or swete with such a noyntement [an ointment]
conditur aromate, hyt ys made savery
conditus . . . media producta, wel[e] savyrd

Folio 158a

media correpta, wel ordeynyd
conduco . . . loco, to sett to hyre
cond[u]cere sodales, to bryng forthe felowys [fellows, companions]
con[?], to a corde [accord, bring into agreement]
conficio . . . conmisceo, to menge [mix, combine]
conuenio . . . pango, make a counawnte
conuenit, hyt semyth [it is fitting]
oportet, hyt be howyth [it behooveth]
rapio, rawysche or to be nomme [*MED, benimen*, take, seize]
permando, to a byde
palam esse, be opyn

Folio 158b

conor, enforce
effero, to bere owte
euenire, to happe [occur]
pasco, fede
cantus . . . spens rote, a spoke of a whele [*spens*, perhaps *spes*; no satisfactory sense is to be found (or for *rotus* as spoke)]
canticum, a songe [subentry]

Folio 159a

dactvlus . . . fructus arboris, a date [Lat.: "est digitus pes"]
dragma . . . pondus, a wyȝth, the viij. parte of an ownce [*wyȝth*, weight]
dictator . . . officium di[c]tandi literas, to endyte lettyrs
discus . . . quidam ludus, a coyte, a dysche [*coyte*, quoit; *dysche*, partly deleted]
parapsis, a platyr [subentry]

Folio 159b

dolus . . . fraus, a gyle
deficio . . . fatiscor, to fayle
resspuo, to for sake or to dysseyve [subentry]
deuoueo . . . spondeo, to be hyte [promise]
maledico, to curse
deuotus . . . execratus, cursyd
benignus, softe and gode [subentry]
diruo . . . demolior, distroy
rodo, gnawe
paro, to a ray [array]

Folio 160a

aliquis certans deponit, with batayle [something omitted? to decide something by means of battle]
aliquis rem commendans in custodia deponit, to take a thyng to kepe
aliquis ministrans cibum vel potum coram aliquo deponit, serwythe forthe
depositor, he that wagythe batayle, a setter of metis, id est sewer in a halle [subentry; sewer, attendant at meals]
depono predictor, a thyng I take to kep
depositarius est ille cui minis-

trantur edenda, he þat ys seruyd or sett in halle
dispono, ordeyne
dissoluere cibum, to defye mete [*MED*, *defien*, v. (2), to digest]

Folio 160b

diluo . . . inscriuo, make stedfast [*MED*, no entry s.v. *make*]
distempero . . . purgo, make clene
dispenso . . . preuidere expensas, ordeyne costis
miserero, have mercy or to dyspence with a man [subentry; *MED*, *dispensen*, 2., administer or impose penance]
edilis . . . custos domus, a ho[w]se keper
curilus, the mere of a towne [subentry; *mere*, mayor; *MED* records sp. *mere*]
euentus . . . casus, chawnce
electrum . . . species gummi, a maner of gumme
species metalli, pewter [subentry]

Folio 161a

emus . . . canor, a spelyng or a syngyng [*OED*, *spelling*, sb.[3], incantation]
erugo . . . rubigo, ruste
estus . . . amor . . . feruor, the boyling of the see
calor, hete [subentry]
examen . . . collectio apum, a swarme of bene [bees; *examen* = *exagmen*]
lingua bilancis, the tonge of a balance [subentry]
acies, the schylterne of a batayle [subentry; *schylterne*, *OED*, *sheltron*, close, compact body of troops; does not record this sp.]
iudicium, the examinacion of the dome [subentry; judgment]
emulor . . . ortor, to hote or commawnde [*hote*, command, promise]
essere . . . insinuare, to schewe

Folio 161b

exanclo . . . haurio in super, to drawe vpp
exhibeo . . . demonstro . . . presento, to present
alo, to norysche [subentry]
dare abunde, to geve pletuosely [subentry; *pletuosely*, error for *plent-*]
exigit . . . exquiro, to aske
iaculor, to caste a darte [subentry]
excipio . . . effero, to bere owte
expedio . . . manifesto, to make opynne

Folio 162a

falx . . . instrumentum cum quo vites amputantur, an hoke
quoddam instrumentum metendi, a sekell [subentry]
quoddam instrumentum falcandi, a sythe [subentry]
facelus . . . cimba, a lytyll bote
quoddam genus legeminis, a maner of potage [subentry; *legeminis*, error for *legu-*; Lat.: "fatum, sorores fatales, viz. gloto, lachesis, antropus"]

Folio 162b

euentus rerum, a chaunce
fedus . . . pignus, a conuawnte [error for *counawnte* (covenant); Lat.: ferula est quoddam instrumentum ligneum quo utuntur magistri in scolis a palmes ("ferrule, a wooden instrument that masters in schools use on the palms of the [students'] hands")]; see *ferula* , fol. 305b.
ficus . . . morbus, a syknesse

frutus, a fygge

Folio 163a

finis . . . destruccio, wastyng
consummacio . . . completum vel adest operi, an endyng [subentry]
finis piperis est calefacere, worschyng [subentry; not in *OED*; perhaps related to *wersh*, a., sickly; *fines . . . calefacere*, "the purpose of pepper is to heat,"]
exluminitas lune, an ende [subentry]
fines sunt regiones proprie indoles possessiones, bowndes [subentry; *bowndes*, bounds, boundaries]
focus . . . foco, a herthe stone
in focario, in the fyre [subentry]
frons, a forhede
fornix . . . lupanar, a bordelle howse
color fucus, a faynte colowre
deceptio, a diseyvyng [subentry]
fungus . . . boletus, todestole

Folio 163b

furfur . . . purgacio farine, the clensyng of mele
futilis . . . homo dicitur futilis quia nihil selare, to keuyr [*MED*, *coveren*, 11 a. (a), to hide: *selare* = *c-*]
facio . . . libo, to do sacrifyce
noceo, to noye [subentry; *noye*, harm, torment, trouble, distress]
facinus . . . factum, a dede
zelus, synne or corsydnesse [subentry]
fero . . . gero, to bere

Folio 164a

effero . . . ferro funus, to bere a corse [subentry; *corse*, corpse]
confero . . . loquor, speke
defero . . . honoro, worschyppe

Folio 164b

differo . . . disto, to be be twene
ferculum . . . companagium certum, a messe of mette [*companagium*, relish, something eaten with bread]
cathedra, a chayr [subentry]
fingo . . . simulo, to feyne

Folio 165a

fundo preces . . . propino, to drawe [*MED* records no appropriate senses (pour out prayers or drink one's health)]
flagro . . . facit ardorem, bornyng [burning]
fragror . . . largitur odorem, to smell swette [*odorem*, altered from *ardorem*]
galla . . . cresta galli, a kombe of a cokke
pomum siluerestis, an oke appyll [subentry; *oke appyll*, oak gall; *siluerestis*, error for *siluestris*]
glans . . . fructus quedam quercus, an akorne
grauis . . . ponderosum, hewy
vox dicitur grauis vel depressa, a lowe woys [subentry]
feminam dicitur grauis vel grauidus, -a [subentry; glossed on next leaf]

Folio 165b

with chylde
graue . . . molestum, grewoys [grievous]
gracia . . . fauor, helpe
gratus . . . naturalis, kyndelyche [naturally]
gratulor . . . letor, to ioy
regracior, to thanke [subentry]
genus . . . stirps, a kynrede
modus, a costome [subentry; *cos-*

tome, custom]
natura rei, a kynde [subentry]
maneres, a maner

Folio 166a

glis . . . animal [illegible] **in noctem,** a dormowse [Lat.: "glires dicti sunt parua animalia, id est tales mures stertunt, id est dormunt toto brumali tempore et viuunt et vigilant estiuo tempore" ("*glires* are small animals that snore like mice, that is they sleep in the winter but wake and live in the summer")]
argilla, cley [subentry]
lappa, a burre
glisco . . . adcresco, to wexe [wax, grow]
glos . . . vetus signum splendens in nocte, a glowtre [not in *MED*; Lat. = an ancient sign shining in the night]
lingua, a tonge [subentry]
gloriam, ioy
gero . . . facio, to doo
gestio . . . cupio . . . gaudeo . . . proprie cum motu corporis, to gett [beget; Lat. = with the appropriate motion of the body]
ibis . . . quedam auis [illegible] **quo rostro purgat posteriora,** [glossed on next leaf; Lat. = a bird that cleans its rear with its beak]

Folio 166b

a storke
ibex, a roo [roe]
auis aquatica serpentum inimica id est quidam serpens, an addyr [subentry]
mineus, envyouse [subentry]
iacinctus, blew bottyll [not in *MED*; blue-bottle (fly?) glossed in another hand]
iuga . . . instrumentum vel primis curris, a ȝoke
lignum in quo voluuntur tele, skey brede [subentry; Lat. suggests part of a loom (the wood on which the cloths turn); *tela*, weaver's beam; *MED*, *bred*, n. (2), board, plank; perhaps *skey* is missing a nasal-bar brevigraph and is an error for *skeyn*, or perhaps it is an error for *sley*]

Folio 167a

indiuiduum . . . nomen proprium, vt: iohannes wyllmus
inuestis . . . expers vestibus, with owte clothys
aliquis sine barba, vt puer vel mulier, berdlese [subentry; *berdlese*, beardless]
vacuum . . . vanus, holowe [subentry]
leuis, lyght [subentry]
immanis . . . ferus, cruel
nocens, noyng [subentry; *noyng*, destructive, threatening]

Folio 167b

improbus . . . perseuerans, a bydyng
ignominiosus . . . ignobilis, worschyppfull [scribe provides an antithetical gloss; the Lat. means, of course, *without* worship or honor]
instita . . . vestis matrone, a roket [*OED*, *rochet*, smock, frock, cloak, or mantle]
vinculum quo pedes mortuoris ligantur, a shete [subentry; *shete*, *OED*, *sheet*, 2., winding sheet]
iacio, to caste
indulgeo . . . dare operam, to ȝeve entent [*MED*, *entent*, b. (a), *given entent*, to take notice]
dare veniam, to for ȝeve [subentry]
infectus . . . maculatus, defowlyde

Folio 168a

latus . . . tegula, a tyle stone
assportatus, borne owte [subentry]
lena . . . pronuba . . . meretrix, a bawde or a strumpete

Folio 168b

lens . . . vermis, a nytte
lentus . . . cessare vel ociari, to be ydyll
flexibilis, bowing [subentry]
lutulentus . . . plenus luto, full of fylth [subentry; *luto,* altered from *pluto*]

Folio 169a

liber . . . vir sine compede natus, a fre man
codex, a boke [subentry]
pars interior . . . suber arboris, the hert of a tre
libra . . . bilanx, a balance [subentry]
pondus, a wyght [subentry]
lictor . . . assecla pretoris, a seruant or a sariant
senus funeris, a hangman or a tormentowre [subentry]
livor . . . lesio, a hurtyng
sanies, fylthe [subentry]

Folio 169b

lira . . . sulcus, a forowe
loculus . . . libitina . . . feretrum, a bere [bier; see fol. 14b]
lupus . . . animal, a wolfe
piscis, a luys [subentry; *luys,* luce]
lego . . . diuidere bona, to be quethe
lego . . . recito, vt clericus legit autores, id est recitat, redythe
furor, to stele [subentry]
vt fur legit, -es, mony [subentry]

Folio 170a

libo . . . gusto, to taste
luo . . . pignusere, I by a ȝen my thyng with mony [redeem]
salio, to skyppe [subentry]
aliud animal salitur in tempore generandi, -is, a sawte [perhaps *OED, sault,* which refers to animals leaping, but there is no appropriate sense provided; perhaps *OED, salt,* a.[2], in heat]
lustrum . . . spacium quique amoris . . . cubile feraris, a cowche
lustro . . . circuo, to go a bowte

Folio 170b

lutum . . . cenum, fylthe
lutosus, folle [subentry; something omitted; full of filth?]
quidam color, scarlett [subentry]
machina . . . res pertinens ad bellum, engyne of batayle
rota, a whele [subentry]
macula . . . tabes, a spotte
foramen in rethe, a hole in a nette [subentry]
manus . . . cetus, a company
membrum corporis, a hande [subentry]
exercitus, an hoste
manica [glossed on next leaf]

Folio 171a

quedam pars in veste, a slefe [sleeve]
maniplus . . . quedam pars illius galie dicitur geline, an handfull of corne
claue, a mase [subentry; *mase, MED, mass,* mass of metal]
cliens, a serwant [subentry]
merges, a grype [subentry; *MED, grip,* n. (3), griffin, vulture]
manipulus dicitur ferreus id est

claua, a masse [subentry]
hoc pilum que solet mittere manu pila, dartis
mena . . . piscis, a menew [minnow]
merges . . . auis, a dewhopper [perhaps *dewdopper*; neither is in *MED* in the sense of a bird; *MED, deubert,* name for the hare (has var. *deuhoppere*); *mergus,* diver (bird)]
garba, a scheffe
maniplus, or a repe of a sheffe [reap(ing) of a sheaf]
milium . . . quedam granum gallice, grumbyll sede [*grumbyll, MED, gromil,* gromwell (*Lithospermum officinale*), no sp. *-b-*]

Folio 171b

nomen numerale, a thowsande [also glosses *milium,* previous leaf]
mithos . . . filum, a threde
queddam nobile sericum, samite [subentry]
iacob dedit filio suo vestem polimitam . . . polimitapola, a gold hoppe [interlinear; meaning is multicolored (Joseph's coat); *MED* has no appropriate entry s.v. *hoppe*]

Folio 172a

molaris, a cheke tothe
lapis, a myll stone [subentry]
momentum, a stounde [moment; Lat.: "quedam pondus sive diuidia vncia vel impressio in denarie"; also "hic mundus equatur ad iij, id est que firmamentum, et id est mundus minor, id est homo, et id est que machina mundi," illustrating the micro-, macrocosm concept which draws parallels between earth and man (*mundus minor*) and between both these and the "universe" (*machina mundi*)]
monumen . . . scriptum, a wrytyng
monumentum . . . sepulcrum, a tomb[e]
moneta . . . numificia, the prynt of mony
moror . . . laudo vel appricio, to worscyppe
retardor, to be taryed [subentry]

Folio 172b

miror . . . laudo, to preyse
misteo . . . propino, byrle [*MED, birlen,* to serve drink]
murmurare, gruche [grumble]
minime . . . aduerbium qualitatis, a lytyll
molior . . . molo, grynde
mollio, make softe
nequicia . . . facinus, vykkydnesse (luxuria)
nepos . . . cognatus, a cosyn

Folio 173a

nisus . . . auis, a hauke
conamen, an enforsyng [subentry]
nota . . . noticia, knowyng
distincio, departyng [subentry; *departyng,* making distinctions]
probum, schame [subentry]
macula vel labes, a spott [subentry]
nomen . . . grauitas, sadnesse [seriousness]
actio, a dede [subentry]
appellacio hominis vel alianus rei, vt iohannes [subentry]
noxa . . . gerenoxa, ed est epialtes, the mare [nightmare; Lat. = Gk. *hiera nósos,* sacred disease, epilepsy]
a distinctionem camporis vel commitatuum, a mere or a cher mere [subentry; *mere,* apparently = *mayor,* noble mayor; *MED, cher,* 1. (b) worthy, esteemed, noble; perhaps = *charmere,* one who casts spells]

Folio 173b

nudus . . . pauper, a pore man
expers vestibus, with owte clothys [subentry]
numerus . . . talus, a dyse [die, one of a pair of dice]
oda . . . sinodus, a seyne [net (?); *sinodus* refers only to synods; Lat. continues: "congregatio presbiteroris"; *seyne* may be an error for *seynod*; see fol. 67b]
officium . . . introitus, a goyng
sermone, a serves or an offys [subentry]
occasio . . . caus, a fallyng [*caus*, error for *casus*]
causa, a chesun [subentry; *chesun*, *MED*, *chesoun*, reason, cause]

Folio 174a

ortus . . . scribitur *h*, hortus, a garden
origo, a spryngyng forthe
natus, borne [subentry]
ora . . . scribitur cum *h*, diei vel noctis, a tyde [time, period of time]
os, a mowthe, a bone [scribe distinguishes *os*, *oris*; *os*, *ossis*]
ocillum . . . paruum os . . . ludus cum fune, a tothyryngame [not in *OED*; apparently a game played with rope (called "little mouth"?); Lat. continues: "Ocillum dic os minimum funis quoque ludum quo se de more portant per mane puelle" (above: "id est puer"); possibly jump-rope; *tothyryng* might be an error for *te-*]

Folio 174b

oro . . . causor, to plete [plead, in court]
causator, a pleter [subentry]
deprecacio, causatio, a pletyng [subentry]
oraculum . . . diuinaculum, id est vaticinium, prophesy [prophecy]
sompnus, a metyng in slepe [subentry; *metyng*, *MED*, *meting*, prophetic or monitory dream]
obuio, mete
alloquor, speke to [subentry]
morior, dye [subentry]
circumeo, to to goo a bowte [subentry; *to* repeated by error]
oblitus . . . fuscatus, made blakke
viciatus, i made fowle [subentry; **i made**, past part.]
oblino, dawbe [subentry]
oblitus, to for ȝett [subentry]
obliuiscor, to for ȝett [subentry; repeated; the previous gloss should probably be *forgotten*]
occido, cado, to slyde or to falle
interficio vel gladeor, slee [subentry; *slee*, slay]
occurro, venire in mentem, to comm to mynde

Folio 175a

obuio, mete
occupo, intendo, take hede
impedio, to lett [subentry; *lett*, prevent]
horreo, metuo, drede [subentry]
rubeo, be aschamyd [subentry]
esse aserpum, to be sharpe or to be grymme in lokyng [subentry]
horripilacio, the stondyng of a mannys here [subentry; Lat.: "Milo transpositum, olim"; following this are Latin mnemonic verses, e.g., "Palma manus palma arbor victoria palma / Palma notat laudem belli victoria finem"]
palma, pars manus, the pame of the honde
arbor, a palme tre [subentry]

Folio 175b

palpa, cecus, blynde
adulator, a gloser [subentry; *gloser*, flatterer]
planeta . . . stella erratica, a planett in the firmament [Lat.: "quedam vestis laxa circa oras (chasuble); septem planeta: saturnus, iupiter, mars, sol, venus, mercurius, luna; luna est propinquissime terre et infimus planetaris et saturnus est remotissimus planetaris a terra et supprimus planetaris"]
planta . . . quelibet herba vel frutex vel arbor que plantatur de nouo in orto vel in agro, a plante [Lat.: *planta pedis* (sole of the foot)]

Folio 176a

pectem . . . piscis, a plays [plaice]
instrumentum lottis, a wesbetyll [interlinear; *wesbetyll*, *OED*, *wash*, VII. 20, wash beetle, instrument for beating clothes]
instrumentum textricis vel textoris quo tele densantur, a glythe [subentry; *glythe*, not in *MED*, *OED*; the Lat. explains it as an instrument for pushing threads together, "condensing" them; see *sley*, fol. 322a]
instrumentum [?] cithare, a wreste [subentry; *wreste*, *OED*, wrest, sb.[5], tuning-key]
instrumentum colonis, a rake [subentry]
instrumentem quo crines plectuntur, a combe [subentry]
lanugo pubes id est prima barba et est prima barba et est ipsam pubes, the schare [subentry; *schare*, groin, pubic area]
corea, a dawnce [subentry]
ordo chori, the ordyr of a quere [choir]

Folio 176b

pernix . . . neco, to sle [slay]
velox, swyfte [subentry]
pernitor, enforce [subentry]
perior . . . experior, to asay
perio, peryche [subentry]
diues, ryche [subentry]
sponsor, a be hoter [subentry; *be hoter*, *MED*, *bihoter*, sponsor]
mediator, a goer betwene [subentry]
princeps, duke or a worthy prynce [subentry]

Folio 177a

[Illegible line]
pila . . . pes pontis, the fote of a brigge
quidam ludus, a ball [subentry]
instrumentum in coquina, a pestell [subentry]
crinis, a here [subentry]

Folio 177b

[Folio bound in codex in inverted position]
populus . . . arbor, a populer [poplar]
collectio hominum vel mulierum, a gederyng of pepyll [subentry]
proximus meus, confinus meus, a neybore [subentry]

Folio 178a

puer . . . purus, clene
pubes . . . illa pars corporis, the schare [groin, pubic area]
pullus . . . fetus, a colte
fetus galline, a chekynne [subentry]
ater . . . niger, blake or derke [subentry]
palus, a stake
palo . . . cauo, to make holow
concauitas anuli in qua gemma

crispatur, the hole of a bond or of a rynge [subentry; *bond, MED, bond,* does not include the sense of "band" or "ring"]
purgo, to [continued on next leaf]

Folio 178b

clense
palea, duste
dare palam, to ȝeve opynly [subentry]
palatum, the rofe of the mowthe [subentry]
pango . . . cano, syng
mergo, ioyne [subentry]
pacistor, make a counawnte [subentry; *counawnte,* covenant]
paro . . . adquiro, purchas
orno, make fayr [subentry]
emo, to by [subentry]
purgosiant in tollendo pecipoma pomi, to pare an appyll or a pere [subentry]
pareo . . . manifestare, to apere or to besye [*MED, bisen,* look, provide; there is no exactly suitable sense]
obedire, to obey [subentry]
patro . . . luxuriare, to do lechery
facio, to doo [subentry]
plecto . . . flecto, to bow
pendo . . . trutino, to wey in a balance
dare penam . . . soluo, to pay dett [subentry]

Folio 179a

presumo . . . male sumere, to mystake or to take to muche vppon confido, truste
confido, truste [subentry]
presto . . . preualo, to hawe mastrye or to be more worthe
prestiti in preterito . . . accomodo, to lende [subentry]
perdio . . . seduco, to disseyve or to be tray
monstrare, to schew [subentry]
exio, to go owte [subentry]
perditor, a traytor

Folio 179b

puto . . . estimo, to trowe
seco, kutt [subentry]
amputo, kutte [subentry]
questus . . . lucrum, wynnyng
querula, a pleynte [subentry; *a pleynte,* complaint]

Folio 180b

rancor . . . corrupcio carnis, the rest of the flesse [*rest,* not in *OED,* but cf. *resty,* a.[2], stale, rancid; *rancor* also = "corrupcio mentis sive longa ira id est ira iracundia"]
radius . . . bige, a spoke
lumen solis, a sonne beme [subentry]
regula . . . instrumentum liginum, a ruler [*liginum,* error for *lignum*]
norma . . . disciplina, a ryȝth techyng

Folio 181a

reticulum . . . instrumentum piscatorum, a nett
instrumentum mulieris, a calle [subentry; *calle, MED, calle,* net (for the hair)]
nouellus, new [glossed supra]
rudis, bustyschman [*MED, boistous,* crude, ignorant, unmannerly]
indoctus . . . nouus, new [subentry]
restat . . . constat, yt ys certeyne
oportet, hyt be howythe [it behooveth]

Folio 181b

redimo, to by a ȝen or to rawnsum
resensitus . . . renouatus, renewyd
sacer . . . sanctus, holy
sagana, gumme
pannus, saye [subentry; *OED, say,* sb.[1], cloth of fine texture resembling serge]
incantrix, a wyche [subentry; *wyche,* witch]
sal . . . condimentum, salt
sapiencia vel eloquencia, wysdome or fayr speche [subentry]
reprehenciones, reprewyngis [subentry; reprovings, remonstrances]
stagnum . . . stannun . . . quedam species metalli, tynne
stagnum est aqua stans, a standyng watyr [subentry]

Folio 182a

species . . . specumen, specery [not in *OED*, error for *specimen*? *spicery,* spice shop, apothecary's; *specumen,* perhaps error for *speculamen,* an observing]
sanguis . . . progenies, a kynrede
quidam humor, blode [subentry]
sanguis alet corpus, nuryschythe the body [subentry]
stacio . . . portus, a hawyn [haven]
stadium, a forlonge [Lat.: "continens C. et XXV. passus"]
passus, passe [subentry; *passe,* pace]
sensus . . . sentencia, vndyr stondyng
significatio, a mewyng [interlinear; *mewyng, MED, meving,* 5. (d), meaning, sense, import (? error for *mening*); this entry proves that the word existed in its own right and *MED*'s bracketed query can be removed; see Thomas W. Ross, note in *Chaucer Newsletter* 2, no. 2 (Summer, 1980); 11]

Folio 182b

signum . . . vexillum, a baner
strigilus . . . quodam instrumentum cum quo equi terguntur, a hors combe
cratis, a hurdyll [subentry]
scansile, a steropp of tre [wood]
sinus, a bosome
portus, hawyn [subentry]
curuacio, a crokyng [subentry; *crokyng,* crooking, curve, bending]
carbasus, a schyppe [subentry]
arcus, a woute [subentry; *woute,* vault]
stirps . . . radix, a rote [subentry; *stirps* also = *progenies*]

Folio 183a

suparus . . . supari sunt plite in velis, the foldyng in weylys [folding in veils (wimples)]
supra sunt vestes mulierum, rochettis [subentry; *OED, rochet,* smock, frock, cloak, or mantle]
supremus . . . extremus, last
summus, altus, hye [subentry]
suspensus . . . tacitus, styll
dependens, hangyng [subentry]
scandalizo . . . exemplifico, to ȝeve an ensample
derideo, to lawghe to scorne [subentry]
sapio . . . sapidus esse, to be sauery
esse sapiens, to be wyse [subentry]

Folio 183b

sterno . . . fasero, to be hernesch [*MED, harneisen,* harness, caparison a horse, deck]
stramento, to strawe [subentry; *strawe, OED, straw,* v.[2], to provide

with straw]

presterno, to draw adowne or to ouyr towrne [subentry]

soluo . . . reddo, to ȝelde

dissoluo, to vnbynde [subentry]

spondeo . . . plegiare, to borow

subigo . . . soppono, to vndyr putt

suffio . . . suffumigare, to make swete smok[e]

ministrare, to minister [subentry]

suggero . . . suggerit vobis omnia, rownyng [whispering]

aliquam signat in malum vt cum dicitur suggestit eue ad commedend pomum vetidum, the apull for bode [subentry; *for bode*, forbidden]

supero . . . abundo, to be plentuys [plenteous]

Folio 184a

suppeto . . . auxil[io], helpe

suspicio . . . specta sursum, to tayr [not in *OED*; the sense seems to be "to look up"]

suspicari, to hawe suspecion [subentry]

sic . . . sic est, so yt ys

talus . . . decius, a dyse [die, one of a pair of dice]

pars pedis, hele [subentry]

taxillus . . . paruus talus, a lytyll hele

paruus decius, a lytyll deys [subentry]

Folio 184b

taxus . . . melota, a grey [*MED*, *grei*, n. (1), badger]

quedam arbor, a ewtre [subentry; *ewtre*, yew tree]

truncus, a stokke [subentry; *stokke*, tree trunk]

taxo . . . vendere . . . exponere res ad mercatum, to selle

extento, prise a thyng at valuere [subentry; *valuere*, *OED*, *valure*; value; this sp. not recorded]

tessera . . . decius, dyse

torax . . . pectus, brest bone

lorica, haburion [subentry]

licor, licoris [subentry; *licoris*, liquors (?); licorice (?), for which the Lat. is usually *glycyrizza* or *licoricia*]

testudo . . . lira, a balke [*MED*, *balk*, ridge between furrows]

volta cauata et est limax, snale [subentry]

piscis in amne, in the see [subentry]

tumidus . . . inflatus, i bollyd [swollen; *MED*, *bollen*, swell]

Folio 185a

carduus, tesyll [*teasel*; this and some subsequent glosses are written above in a different hand]

palearia, deewlappis [*palearia*, wattles of a cook; *palear*, dewlap of an ox]

titulus . . . epigrama, tytyll

turbus, cappe

tollit . . . leuat, erigit, a reyr [*MED*, *areren*, raise]

Folio 185b

varus . . . curuus, crokyd

vas . . . fidemssor, a borow [*MED*, *borwen*, 2., become surety for; no appropriate entry as a noun]

vehimens . . . vehens, se a mente [error for *vehemente*?]

velum . . . instrumentum nauis, a sayle

instrumentum monialis, a weyle [subentry; *weyle*, veil]

venenum . . . virus, venyme

Folio 186a

verbum . . . decepcio, disseyte
vindicta . . . liberta, fredome
vlcio, veniance [subentry; *veniance*, vengeance]
vir . . . signat probitatem, vt ipse est vir, he is a manlyman
virago . . . magistra viri, the hosbondys master
vola . . . pars ale, the penowne of a wynge
pars pedis, the sole of the fote [subentry]
vber . . . mamma, a tete
fertilis, fertile, plentuys [subentry; *plentuys*, plenteous]
fertilitas, plentuysnesse [subentry; Lat.: "Hic ponit differenciam inter hoc vber, -ris, idem que mamma, a tete, vt in euangelio beata, vbera que suxisti, et hic, hec, hoc vber, -ris, equor ad ij., i.e., hic, hec fertilis et hoc fertile, *plentuys*, et idem est que fertilitas"; the reference to Scripture is apparently to Isaiah 60.16]
vua . . . fructus vitis, grape

Folio 186b

vsus . . . v[alu]tas, profytt
excercicium, hawntyng [subentry; *hawntyng*, *MED*, 2. (a) practice, exercise]
vsus . . . mos, maner or a custome
vaco . . . vacuum esse, to be woyd [void, empty]
valet . . . validum esse, to be strong
vale et valete debent dici homini discedenti . . . et debet dici homini morienti, departyng
valeat, far he well

Folio 187a

verro . . . quoddam instrumentum quo purgatur domus, besome [besom, broom]
sulco, to ere [subentry; *ere*, plow]
varrus, a barrow h[ogge] [subentry]
deleo, to do a way
voco . . . appellare, to name
cido, to somen [subentry; *somen*, summon to court; Lat.: "i.e. aliquis vocat ad iudicium"]
volo . . . pretendo, to schew
optare, desire [subentry]

Folio 187b

vel . . . siue, or whedyr
xenium . . . munus, a ȝefte

Folio 188a

zelus . . . mutacio, folow [illegible]
suspicio, suspecion [subentry]
inuidia, envy [subentry]
Explicit

Folio 192b

[A Latin exercise in which the scholar speaks of spending many years in London and, in the future, of studying grammar at Canterbury or Oxford. These folios contain much talk of schoolboy matters: laziness, lateness, punishment, lack of money, evil companions, drinking, and the need to practice speaking Latin.]

Folio 195a

verecundia, shame

Folio 199a–204b

[A collection of some of the *Distichs of Cato*, concluding with "Explicit liber Catonis, a Warrewyke," suggesting that at least this portion of the manuscript was composed at Warwick]

Folio 244a

[Conclusion of a section on Latin grammar. In a blank space occur these macaronic verses (they are repeated on fol. 275a): "Non est in mundo qui poscit tangere fundum / Clerici quid velles mecum si nocte iaceres / Vellem se velles nostras coniungere pelles / Non sum de illis qui ponunt illud in illis / Sum de illis qui dicunt "do what yowre wyll ys." It is a bawdy, homosexual invitation.]

Folio 255b

[Music. In the margin a sixteenth-century hand notes: "The tune that Alfred played in the Danish camp."]

Folio 267b

[Glosses of Latin verses]
rigidas, styfe
stiterat, stand styll
aggere, brynke [error for *brynge*]
certare, stryve
cedat, go eyn [go in? not clear]
adeo, so myche
quo res cuique, what sum euer maner

Folio 269a

vulcan, smyght [smith]
ciclopes, þe smythye

Folio 269b

Ad me [?] curam pecoris, þat kyng [something omitted]
superbi, nobyl
suber, barke [bark of a tree]
supino, bowyng downe
phillis, a fylbertre [filbert tree]
cavtem, stoke [stock, stump]

Folio 270a

diane, goddes

Folio 272a

I haue wyschyd very oftyn þat I had lernyd to pley on the horgans, on the harpe, and on the lute when I was yowng for by seyd þei be a plesure to them þat haue them, they putt a way heuines, ydyllnes, and teduysnes [*horgans*, organ; commonly pl. in ME; *haue*, altered from *hange*; the entire passage is immediately translated into Latin, beg. "Optam quam sepissime . . ." it was evidently a set piece for translation]

Folio 274a

[Moral maxims, with internal rhyme. Some are not moral but humorous, e.g., "Non sunt felices si matres sunt meretrices" ("they are not happy whose mothers are whores"); and "Optimus est ludus cum virgine nudus / lance carnalis non dat sibi vulnera mortis" ("the best game is nude with a virgin. The lance of flesh does not inflict a mortal wound").]

Folio 275a

[Repeats the macaronic verse on fol. 244a, followed by a mock-Latin passage: "Nomina dyrtorum generis sunt stynkatynorum / De dyrt excepto quod conuenit ori meo." Followed by this English passage, another set exercise which is immediately translated into Latin: "Iohn y know by þi wordys þat þou owyste me no gud wyll / þerfor I hope þat þe master wyll not be lyue þe / when thow complaynyst vn me whyll he fownde no / fawte by me hym selfe." After the Latin translation of the foregoing: "I repent me now euery day mor and mor þat my fadyr and my modyr made so myche of me when y was yong for and they hade lete me of my wyll (kept me from having my way) and desyer as hyt was þer parte y schulde a byn now far cunnynger and yn better case then y am."]

Folio 275b

[Among some Latin: "I haue fownd a snakys skyne."]
obeo, to dye
Ho ys dede yn owr pareche to day [immediately translated: "Quis obeitt hodie in parocha nostra," a useful exercise for a future clerk, who would have to keep parish records of the dead]

Folio 276a

[A passage in Lat. explaining that terms are translated into English for reading and hearing]
hic deus, hic creator pater et filius et spiritus sanctus coniuncti, god
iesus, christus, redemptor, numen, god hede
dominus, omnipotens, cuntipotens, astripotens, altitonans, altisonans, altissimus, altisonus, altisonus, totus deus, tota diuina potestas, panton craton, god almyghty [*cuntipotens,* error for *cuncti-*]
pnuema, paraclitus, consolator, the holy goste [*pnuema,* error for *pneuma*]
deitas, diuinitas, numen, diuinapotestas, diuinamagestas, virtus, deiconunitor, god hede

Folio 276b

mag[nitudo], immensitas, immensurabilitas, vigencia, infinitas, mekenesse [error for *greatness*? alternatively, the last Lat. word may be an error for *infimitas*]
angelus, an angell
nuncius, a messangere
archangelus, an arcangell
celum, polum, olimpus, vranus, paradisus, hewyn
altitudo, celtitudo, magnificencia, summitas, excellencia, sublimitas, culmen, cacumen, apex, hynesse
benignitas, senutas, beneficencia, godnesse
pulcritudo, decor, forma, formositas, species, speciositas, eligancia, fayrnesse
misericordia, clemencia, pietas, propiciacio, miseracio, mercy
compassio, remissio, remedium, relaxacio, releuamen, condonacio, forgevenes[se]

Folio 277a

indulgencia, idem, venia [belong with terms on preceding leaf]
dulcedo, dulcor, odor, suauitas, swettnesse
solamen, solacium, consolacio, consolamen, comfortacio, comfortamen, comfort
melodia, melus, armonia, cantus, camena, canticum, cantilena, carmen, modulacio, modulamen, concentus, musa, a swete songe
symphonia, a symphonye [used vaguely for various stringed instruments]
symphonista, a simphonistar
fidula, a fydyll
ficulacista, a fydler

corus, a crowde [stringed instrument]
coritatuus, a crowder
buccina, tuba, sistrum, lituus, a trumpe
tibicen [not glossed, = flutist]
cithera, lira, testudo, a harpe
citharedus, liricen, a harper
timpanum, a tabyr
timpanista, a taberer
simbalum, a symballe
simbalista, a symbaler
psalterium, a sawtery
nabulum, a naker [kettledrum; however, *nabulum,* a kind of harp]
organum, an organne
organista, an organer
fistula, cantescium, tuba, a pype
fistulacista, a pyper

Folio 277b

cornu, cornucium, a cornet
cornicen, a cornerer [error for *corneter*]
vnitas, vnanimitas, congruitas, consumitas, consonancia, cordyng
plenitudo, sufficiencia, abundancia, fertilitas, fecunditas, copiositas, affluencia, vbertas, copia, opimitas, opilencia, plente
possessio, facultas, faceos, substancia, suiicie, gracie, thesaurus, locupletacio, census, catallum, ryches
datum, datom, donum, donacio, donatium, munus, munusculum, largicio, collacio, exhibicio, tributum, errogacio, a gyfte
gracia, gratitudo, caristia, carisma, a grace
caritas, amor, dilectio, affectus, affectatio, amicicia, [glossed on next leaf]

Folio 278a

zelus, love
amicus, dilectus, a frende
desiderium, votum, adeptacio, electio, appetitus, a desyre
veritas, veracitas, fides, bothe [apparently refers to *truth* and *tryst,* which follow]
fidelitas, truthe
fiducia, fiducialitas, tryst
securitas, firmitas, stabilitas, constancia, sykyrnesse
defencio, tutacio, timiaium, protectio, a defendyng
custodia, tutela, pusris, pusura, regimine, obseruancia, a kepyng
facessia, vrbanitas, curialitas, lepos, curtesye
humilitas, mitercia, mansuetudo, deuocia, simplicitas, examinacio, subiectio, prostratio, submissio, obediencia, reuerencia, virtus, mos, a vetu [error for *vertu*; *prostratio,* corr. from *-actio*]
paciencia, longanimitas, tollerancia, iusticia, sufferyng [*iusticia* belongs with next group]

Folio 278b

ius, rectitudo, equitas, ryght
robu[r], fortitudo, vis, vigor, visus, vires, strenkyth
conamen, potestas, potencia, dicio, nutus, munem, facultas, valitudo, myght [*hardynesse* deleted]
audacia, magnanimitas, animositas, hardynesse
prudencia, intelligencia, austucia, calleditas, cautela, wontenesse [error for something like *care, caution*]
solercia, dolus, industria, warnesse [cautiousness, vigilance]
sapiencia, musa, minna, sub-

tilitas, Apollo, wysdome
baducia, facultas, conyng
sensus, sentencia, intellectus, ingenium, discretio, wytt
iudicium, preiudicium, examen, sensura, arbitrium, dome [judgment]
ratio, lex, calculus, skyll

Folio 279a

animus, idem [glosses the items in the preceding entry]
voluntas, velle, nutus, animus, placitum, [?] umplacitum, libitum, benevolencia, wylle [(?)*umplacitum* blotted]
temporancia, moderacio, moderancia, modestia, mensuracio, modus, sobria, sobrietas, parcimonia, frugalitas, mesure [moderation]
continencia, castitas, pudor, pudicicia, castimonia, integritas, chastite
immundicia, innocencia, impuritas, cinseritas, clennes [*impuritas*, error for *puritas*]
dignitas, autoritas, grauitas, nobilitas, strenua, worthynesse
strenuitas, probitas, idomitas, nobilitas, strenua, [b]owntnesseness[e]
agelitas, subtilitas, efficacitas, tenitas, leuitas, lytenesse
gerositas, proseritas, libertas, fredome [*gerositas*, error for *generositas*; *proseritas*, error for *prosperitas*]

Folio 279b

ingenutas, genietrye [not in *MED*, *OED*; *ingenutas*, error for *-uitas*]
largitas, liberalitas, munificencia, hillaritas, largenesse [generosity]
consilium, pensum, consultacio, consiliaco, consultum, a cownselle [*consiliaco*, error for *-cio*]
adiutorium, adiumentum, auxilium, patrocinium, precidium, subsidium, adiuuinculum, suffragium, refugium, succursus, supportacio, opitulacio, propiciacio, subuencio, a helpe
societas, consorcium, cetus, chorus, cuneus, agmen, collegium, commitina, turba, conuentus, contibernium, conuenticulum, sodalicium, sodalitas, concom, congregacio, caterua, phalanx, legio, socius, consocius, a company

Folio 280a

consors, sodalis, comes, collega, a felowe
tropheum, victoria, triumphus, palma, a victurdome [*OED*, first cit., 1526]
sanitas, firmitas, incolemitas, helthe [*incolemitas*, error for *incolumitas*]
gaudium, leticia, plausus, delyȝthe
exultacio, gratulacio, congratulacio, delectamen, delectamentum, oblectamentum, iubilacio, letacio, onacio, onamen, iubilus, letamen, iocunditas, hillaritas, delicio, amenitas, ioye
vita, animus, statem, a lyfe
immortalitas, eternitas, sempiternitas, durabilitas, perennitas, perpetuitas, longanimitas, longitudo, perseuerancia, longlastyng

Folio 280b

requies, pausa, pausacio, quies, refrigerium, auecis, rest
pax, tranquillitas, pese

honor, decus, laus, titulus, veneracio, precomium, a worshyppe
paratus, apparatus, ornatus, somma, a dyȝtyng [adorning]
sedes, sedile, sella, subsellum, stancium, tronus, soilum, cathedra, agalina, tribunal, suggestus, transtrum, a sete
ordo, regula, disposicio, ordinacio, norma, canon, an ordynnyng
corona, cectum, laurea, auriola, ciruale, apex, diadema, a garland [*cectum,* error for *certum (sertum)*?]

Folio 281a

premium, premiacio, remuneracio, merces, recompensacio, donatium, brauium, mede [gift, payment, sometimes bribery (first four Lat. terms mistakenly included in series glossing *a garland*)]
saluacio, salus, salutare, helthe
prosperitas, fecunditas, media, plentiusnesse
gliam, doxa, beatitudo, felicitas, blys
firmamentum, a fyrmament
sol, phebus, titan, apollo, ipergeus, ipogeus [not glossed]
luna, lucina, phebe, sinthea, the mone
neomenia, nouilunum, the newmone
semilunum, media luna, plenilunium, plena luna [not glossed]
stelle, sidus, astrum, a sterre
planeta, saturnus, iupiter, mars, mercurius, venus, sunt nomina planeta [not glossed]
lucifer, the deysterre
esperus, vesperus, euynsterre
lux, lumen, iubar, claritas, lyȝthe

Folio 281b

claritudo, luculencia, splendor, nitor, radius, radiacio, coruscacio, serenitas, cleyrnesse
fulgor, tradies, bryȝtness [*tradies,* error for *radies*?]
tempus, a tyme
hora, momentis, articulus, an avyr [*hour*]
orilogium, an orlage [*(h)orloge,* clock]
nox, a nyȝthe
vesperum, sero, crepusculum, an euyntyde
continicinium, bedtyme
intempestum, mydnyght
gallicantus, a cokkcrow
aurora, a mornyng
diliculum, mane, matutinum, vespera, mornetyde
aier, ether, aura, an eyr
oriens, the est
occidens, the weste
auster, meridies, the sowthe
borias, aquili, septentrio, the northe
annus, a ȝere
mensis, a monthe
ianuarius, februarius, marcius, aprilis, maius, iunius, iulius, augustus, sunt nomina mensium [not glossed]

Folio 282a

september, october, nouember, december, sunt nomina mensium [not glossed]
nubes, nubecula, nubulum, nebula, a clowde
fulgur, fulmen, coruscacio, fulminacio, lytynnyng
tonitrium, tonitruus, tonitru, thundyr

Nomina Ventorum
[Names of the winds]

ventus, aura, spiritus, spiraculum, spiramen, a wynde
turbo, mipitus, tempestas, procella, a tempest [*mipitus*, error for *mephitus*]
subsolanus, estwynde
austeraifficus, sowthe wyn[de]
fauonius, westernwynde
chorus, northewestwynd
zeferus, westwynde
affricus, sowthewestwynde
circius, ventusborialis [not glossed]
aquilo, versus occidentem . . . [not glossed]
pluuia, imber, nubus, a rayne
grando, hayle
nix, snowe
gelu, a froste
glacies, yse
stiria, an ysehangyll [icicle; not in *MED*]

Folio 282b

gelisidium, liquifactio, thawyng
musicia, a swamwatyr [swamp water ? not in *OED*]
aqua, limpha, vnda, ampius, latex, tecis, a watyr
flumine, fluentum, fluuius, diluuium, cataclismus, a flode
riuus, riuulus, torrens, streme
fons, fontulus, a welle
catharacta, via sub humo [not glossed]
catatipta, conductus terre [not glossed]
scaturigo, ebullio, a wellyng
trochea, a wyndas [*OED*, *windas*, windlass; *trochea*, error for *trochlea*, pulley]
mergo, ripa, litus, a banke
arena, grauell
sabulum, sonde
glaria, sclesell [not in *OED*; *glaria* = gravel, earth]
mare, pontus, salum, equor, fretum, pellagus, vnda, defluctus, see [sea]
fluxus, venalia, a flowyng
refluxus, salaria, ebbyng
portus, portulus, stacio, a hawyn [haven, port]

Folio 283a

De nave et eius pertinencijs
[Of the ship and its appurtenances]

nauis, a schyppe
nauicula, prora, puppis, cimba, simbrus, barca, facelus, lentus, carbasa, ratis, pare, dentis, legis, standia, scapha, a schyppe
galia, a galye
drono, a drone [not in *MED*; some kind of vessel, perhaps akin to *dromond*, galley]
classis, a navy
nauta, nauita, nauclerus, a schyppman
nauigator, remigator, a rower
remex, a steryscheman [steersman]
remus, amplustrum, an ower
foramen [not glossed]
forus, a rother [rudder]
columbar, a hole [see *foramen* (= hole) above; the scribe is searching for oarlock]
malus, maste
ancora, an ankyr
atempna, rudens, cabyll
alne, ventis maris [not glossed]
velum, lintheum, seyle
carchesium, sayleȝerde
allumium, allunes, alluno, alga, oserant [not in *OED*; seaweed?]
vlna, wreke
palus, a maryses [marsh]

Folio 283b

labina, idem [glosses the preceding entry]
vadum, a wayowre [*OED, wayour,* horsepond]
stagium, vmarium, piscina, fyscepole [fishpool, -pond]
fossa, fonda, lacus, lacina, specus, spelunca, strobs, cauea, cubile, lustrum, dyke or a denne [*MED, diche,* 4. (c), cave, den]
estas, somer
hyems, bruma, wynter
ver pars anni qui oram virent, were [Fr. *ver,* spring]
autumnus tum aliquid dicimus Augustus, herwyste [harvest (designating a season]
mundus, orbis, orbis terrarum, the worlde
terra, arida, solum, humus, tellus, the erthe
terremotus, an erthe quake
creta, calx, chalke
gluten, argille, bitumen, lutum, gipsum, clay or plaster
limus, slyme
infernus, tartarus, iehenna, baratrum, erebus, orcus, helle

Folio 284a

auernus, abissus, acheron [glosses previous entry, but Acheron belongs with the rivers of hell]
stix, flagiton, lethes, cochitus, sunt fluuij infernales [not glossed]
diabolus, demon, demonum, cacademon, satanas, satan, belial, lucifer, apostata, pluto, a devyll
profunditas, abissus, depenesse
maledictum, maledictio, excommunicacio, execracio, execretas, detestacio, anatheme, anathemizacio, a curse
obscuritas, opas[itas], caligo, tenebre, obfuscacio, furnitas, derkenesse
malicia, malignitas, prauitas, peruersitas, nequicia, obstinacio, impietas, seueritas, crudelitas, austeritas, feritas, schrewdnesse [cursedness, wickedness]

Folio 284b

ferositas, inhumanitas, idem [glosses previous entry]
vindicta, vlcio, framea, vengeans
amaritudo, acerbitas, acritas, bilis, bilitas, byttyrnesse
turpitudo, feduas, fetor, olor, a stynke
putredo, sanies, tabes, tabecula, pus, inde lege grande tabi, damno[?]tabe, fylthe
impaciencia, femurris, murmuracio, murmur, susurra, gruggyng [grumbling]
sonus, strepitus, tumultacio, noyse
iniusticia, iniuria, iniquitas, error, distorcio, wronge
desolacio, disperacio, diffidencia, wanhope [despair]
heresis, discredencia, incredulitas, mysbeleve
gemitus, fletus, ploratus, suspirium, planctus, vlulatus [glossed on next leaf]

Folio 285a

ploracio, lamentacio, luctus, meror, euilacio, compascio, a waylyng
discordia, disconformitas, disformitas, cisma, contrarietas, rubellio, discensus, dissonancia, discrepancia, sedicio, discorde [*rubellio,* error for *re-*]

fames, esuries, hungyr
sitis, thurste
defectus, paupertas, pouerte
miseria, moria, egestas, pennuria, media, captiuitas, erumpna, necesse, inde lege opus, inde lege necessitas, nede, **odium, inimicia,** hatred, **inimicus, hostis, aduersarius, emulus,** enuy, **mendacium, figmentum,** a lesyng [lie]

Folio 285b

falcitas, fallacia, fraus, tegna, falsenesse [*tegna*, error for *techna(e)*]
dolus, trica, decepcio, seducio, meandere, perdicio, impostura, eleuanns, a gyle
scurrilitas, inurbanitas, rusticitas, stultiloquium, harlatry [*MED*, *harlot*, man of no fixed occupation; hence *-ry* = roguishness, boorishness, foolish (and often obscene) talk]
obprobrium, improperium, vituperium, commaun, stryffe [gloss continued in next column]
iurgium, exprobacio, reprehencio, redargucio, contencio, certacio, altercacio, obiurgacio, certamen, litigium, litagacio, acoma, stryffe
listis, rixa, vpreydyng [upbraiding, scolding]
superbia, elacio, elacio, tumor, fastas [glossed on next leaf; *elacio* repeated by mistake]

Folio 286a

inflacio, extollencia, iactancia, errogancia, pryde
indignacio, despectus, contemtus, contumacio, despyte, gytte [*MED*, *gitten*, *v.*, to vaunt or brag; *despectus*, altered from *di-*]
vicium, peccatum, peccamen, crimen, menda[cio], labes, noxa, culpa, probrum, delictum, piacula, offensio, offensa, synne
re[?]us, scetus, facinus, nephas, voluptas, illecebre, synne, fowlenesse [*scetus*, error for *scelus*]
impotencia, debilitas, imbesilitas, inualitudo, febyllnesse
infirmatas, egretudo, morbus, syknesse
timor, metus, dubitacio, esitacio, formido, pauor, ambiguitas, drede
distruccio, a wastyng [continued on next leaf]

Folio 286b

dissipacio, dilapidacio, diuastcio, a wastyng [*diuastcio*, error for *-acio*]
prodigalitas, superfluitas, owteraiowse [*outrageous* (excessive); error for *-nesse*?]
excessus, stulcia, impaciencia, distinpencia, insciencia, fatuitas, temeritas, presumpcio, ignorancia, ignarua, baba, foly
gula, gulositas, ingluuies, commesacio, letacitas, glotony [continued in next column]
crapula, castrimergia, gloteny
elluo, bucco, lurco, mando, gluto, gulo, nebulo, ardelio, etro, commedo, epulo, neperhas, parasitus, lecator, ambro, vorator, deourator, traneo, commessator, a glotun
luxuria [continued on next leaf]

Folio 287a

luxus, incontinencia, impudicicia, fornicacio, adulterium, adulteracio, incestus, incestus, peculencia, peculacio, laciuia, venus, lechery [*incestus* repeated by mistake]

immundicia, impuritas, inhonestas, ignobilitas, improbitas, inprobitas, vnclennesse

grauitas, gravitudo, puder[?], hewynes [heaviness; also torpor, drowsiness, dullness]

pigricia, desidia, accidia, torpor, torpedo, slownesse

seruitus, serenitas, illibertas, thraldome [corrected from *fredome*; *serenitas* is out of place in the series; it is perhaps an error for *seueritas*, condition of being hardened by toil]

auaricia, cupitas, cupido, tenacitas, fragelctas, concupriscencia, suggestio, visitacio, vocctamentum, procuracio, eggyn [*MED*, *eggen*, entice, lure; *fragelctas*, error for *fragilitas*; *concupriscencia*, error for *concupi-*]

Folio 287b

dolor, tristicia, mestus, mesticia, molestia, angustia, tribulacio, aduersitas, anxietas, sorowe

prostacio, degestio, digestio, deiectio, depressio, oppressio, coniunctio, conculcacio, subpeditacio, a defoulyng

labor, sudor, labowre

vexamen, vexacio, infestacio, inquietacio, trawell [travail]

nocumentum, tedium, fastidium, noysumnesse [annoyance, tediousness]

mors, letum, nomino caret ergo huiquecis, obitus, interritus, interempcio, interfectio, occiso, clades, pernicies, necacio, pestis, mortificacio [continued on next leaf]

Folio 288a

decessus, cedes, pestilencia, mortalitas, morticinium, a dethe

bellum, duellum, prelium, pugnacio, pugna, conflictus, conflictacio, impugnacio, obpugnacio, a batayle

dedicus, inhoracio, irreuerencia, dishonowre

tormentum, tortura, a tormentyng [continued in next series]

cruciatus, cruciamen, exciaum, flagellum, flagellacio, afflictio, a tormentyng [*exciaum*, error for *excruciatum* or possibly *excidium*]

verber, verberamen, verbaracio, percucio, betyng

insania, furor, furia, vesania, amencia, demencia, rabies, frausis, baccania [continued on next leaf]

Folio 288b

terto, energia, amencia, wodnesse [madness; *terto*, error for *tor-*?]

cruciator, lictor, exactor, speculator, a tormentowre

ignis, igniculus, focus, pir, rogus, fyyr

calor, estus, estuacio, incendium, adustio, combustio, arsura, caminus, hete

frigus, colde [continued in next series]

frigiditas, gelitas, tepeditas, frigor, frigencia, frigucies, tremor, colde

pena, penalitas, multa, multacio, ardilla, punicio, luicio, animadversacio, redempcio, a rawnsome [*ransom*, redemption; it glosses only the last term, *redempcio*; the other terms require a gloss like *punishment*; *ardilla* added in a later hand]

morsus, morsio, morsura, a bytyng or a gnawyng

remedium, irrifugium, irrecuperacio, a remedy

Folio 289a

principium, inicium, exordium, primordium, a begynnyng
natura, genus, a kynd
progenies, sanguis, tribus, parentela, propago, stirps, sol[?]les, proles, prosapia, indolex, generacio, nacio, genitura, genesis, a kynrede
[Illegible line]
anus, a belsyre
ania, a beldame
patruus, auunculus, an eme [uncle]
amita, matertera, an awnte
patruelis, id est filius vel filia martertere vel sunt adiectiua [not glossed; similarly, several of the subsequent terms for kinship are left unglossed]
pater, parens, genitor, generator, a fadyr
paternitas, fadyrhede
parens, mater, genitris, genetrix, a modyr
compater, paternus, a godefadyr

Folio 289b

commater, commaterna, a godmodyr
filiolus, a godsun
filiola, a goddowter
patriaster, victricus [not glossed]
nouerca, patriasta, a steppe modyr
filius, natas, pignus, a sonne
filia, nata, proles, a dowghter
filialitas, sonnhede
filiaster, prenignus, a stepsonne
filiastra, prenigna, stepdowtyr
pelex id est mulier coniuncta a viro sub vxore [*pelex,* concubine]
pelignus, filius eius [subentry]
peligna, filia eius, a horcoppe [subentry, *MED, horcop,* bastard]
frater, germanus, brothyr
fraternitas, brodyrhede
consobrinis filius sororis
consobrina filia sororis [subentry]
patruelis est fratris vel est adiectiuum, [subentry, *fratris,* altered from *patris*]
congnatus, nepos, a cosyne
cognata, neptis, a nese
affinis, a kynnysman
sponsus, maritus, coniunx, howsbonde
vxor, sponsa, a wyfe [continued on next leaf]

Folio 290a

nupta, coniunx, a wyfe
domiduca, a breyde [bride]
coniugium, copula, maritagium, sponsale, impcidaris, a weddyng [**impcidaris,** error for *impeditio*?]
socer pater sponsi et sponse, eldyr fadyr, eldyr modyr
socrus mater sui et sue
gener vel sponsus filie [subentry]
nurus vxor filij [subentry]
sorarius sponsus sororis [subentry]
glos sponsa fratris [subentry]
imperator, an emperowre
imperatrix, a empresse
rex, regulus, princeps, a kynge
regina, a quene
dux, a duke
ducissa, duchesse
comes, erle
commitissa, cowntesse
baro, baron
baronissa, baronesse
miles, eques, knyte
principatus, commitatus, baronitt, munericia, dominium sunt dignitatores predictorum [not glossed]

Folio 290b

[Illegible line]
dominus, erus, magnas, lorde
heres, primeris [not glossed]

domina, era, lady
domicellus, dominellus, armiger, squyer
domicella, dominella, damselle
paterfamilias, iconomus, a howsebonde
iconomia, husbondrye
pergula, domus, familia, a meyny [retinue, household]
famulus, seruus, seruulus, minister, serwant
verna, verniculus, assecla, cliens, empticius, pusio, garcio, pedisecus, a man serwant
famula, serua, seruicula, ancilla, pedisequa, abra, a woman seruante
seruicium, famulatus, ministerium, obsequium, officium, nuncium, clientela, a serwyse

Folio 291a

natiuitas, ortus, origo, natale, natalis, a byrthe
precus, puerperium, a childyng
infans, infantulus, puer, puerulus, a chyld
infantula, puerula, puella, a wenche
virgo, virginicula, a wyrgynne [virgin]
iuuenis, adolescens, adolescentulus, a yong man
adolescentula, iuuencula, a yong woman
vir, homo, homunculus, homuncio, mas, masculus, antrapos, microsmus, a man [*microsmus*, error for *microcosmus*]
senex, decrepitus, an olde man
mulier, muliercula, femina, virago, femella, a woman
anus, vetula, an olde wyffe
infancia, chyldhode

Folio 291b

puericia, chyldhode
adolescentia, indoles, iuuentus, iuuenta, youthe
virilitas, humanitas, manhodde [*humanitas*, added in later hand]
senectus, senecta, senum, decrepitudo, etas, etacula, enum, age [*senecta*, corr. from *senestra*]
nutritor, fetor, alunnus, educator, nutrix, fotrix, alunna, educatrix, a nurysche [nurse]
nutricia, educaria, alunnaria, a nuryschyng [nourishing]
cunabulum, cunearis, crepundium, a cradyll
fassia, fassiola, a cradylbonde
crepundiaria, quatitaria, fassenaria, a rokker [*OED*, *rocker*, 1., one who rocks (a cradle)]
fassine, a lullyng
orixorium, saliuarium tersorium, a slaueryng clowte [slavering cloth (bib); not in *OED*; first cit. for *slavering*, sixteenth century]
saliua, sputum, spetull
muccus, politis, carenrus, snevyll [snivel, mucus]

Folio 292a

caterrus, corisa, the pose [head cold]
reuma, reme [rheum; *OED* does not record this sp.]
tussis, disma, the cowght
anima, animus, mens, spiritus, mensio, meditacio, cogitacio, excogitacio, reminiscencia, recolencia, memoria, a mynde
atadummus, calculus, a skyll
corpus, corpusculum, body
membrum, artus, lymme
caput, capitulum, capitellum, cephas, a hede [for this and subsequent entries, see parallels beg. fols.

7b and 309a]
pilus, capillus, crinis, coma, cezeries, an here
iuba, diuisio, discrimen, the schede of the here [part (division) of the hair]
glabra, glabella, discrimen, a scall [corr. from *sch-*; *OED, scall,* scaly or scabby disease
cinciput, a nodyll [*MED, nodel,* back of the head]
interciput, id est media pars capitis [not glossed]
occiput, seruix, a haterelle [*MED, haterel,* n. (1) (c), back of the head]
cranium, the braynepanne

Folio 292b

cerabrum, the brayne panne
cerabrum, cerabellum, breyne [*cerabrum,* repeated]
frontinellum, nekkpytt [depression at base of neck]
auris, aricula, ere
frontinella, frotenula, forhede
supercilium, palpebra, an ylyd [eyelid]
cilium, the ouyr browe
oculus, ocellus, tolunus, an ye
visus, visio, acies, the syȝthe
pupilla, appyll of the ye
glauconia, grownd of the ye
albucies, albedo, glaucitas, whyte of the ye
ircus, subircus, the whyte of the ye [repeated]
nasus, nose
purila, punila, poynt of the nose
cartilago, brystyll of the nose [*brystyll,* error for *gr-*; scribe's eye-skip to *brygge* (below)?]
naris, a nostrelle
intersinuum, brygge of the nose
labrum, labellum, labium, lyppe
os, ocellum, bucca, buccula, mowthe
dens, tothe

Folio 293a

dentulus, molaris, geminius, a wange tothe [cheek tooth (canine)]
gingiua, lingua, lingula, glossa, tonge [*gingiua, gingiva,* gum (of the mouth)]
verbum, loquela, vox, dictio, locutio, omelia, predicacio, lingua, sonus, dictum, sermo, colloquium, famen, lingua, a word or a speche [*lingua,* repeated]
idioma, langage
palatum, rofe of the mowthe
isophogus, a wesande [windpipe]
epiglottum, a throte bolle [throat boll, larynx]
mandula, mandubula, cheke bonne
faux, branca, mentum, chynne
mala, maxilla, gena, cheke
mentum, mentulum, chynne [repeated]
barba, berde
columna, collum, nekke
facies, faciecula, face

Folio 293b

vultus, chere [visage]
effigies, similitudo, lyknesse
guttur, gula, iugulus, brancus, gurgulie, throte
scapula, humerus, armus, an arme
ala, acella, arme hole [armpit]
lacertus, id est superior pars vlna, a brachir [*MED, brache,* n. (2), measure of arm's length, an ell; no sp. in *-ir, -er*; the Lat. indicates that *brachir* was thought of as the upper (or fore) part of the arm, not as a measure]
cubitus, elbowe
cubitus anterior pars brachij cum qua mensura vlna [not glossed]
manus, hande [continued in next col-

umn]
palma, vola, ir, hand [*ir, hir*]
pugnus, pugillus, fyste [*pugillus*, added above, same hand]
condolus, fragus, knokyll
palmus, spanne
digitus, fynger
pollex, index, medius, medicus, auricularis, sunt nomina digitoris [not glossed]
pulpa, pulpula, lyre [*MED*, *lire*, n. (2), flesh]
lauerna, fixfax [*MED*, large tendon in neck of animal]
runca, runkyll [*OED*, *runkle*, wrinkle, crease; *runca*, perhaps error for *ruga*]
iuctura, compago, compages, ioyntures [*iuctura*, error for *iunc*-]

Folio 294a

neruus, a sinew
vena, artaria, vayne [altered from *w*-]
vnguis, vngula, anayle [written as one word]
torax, brest bone
mamma, mamilla, vber, papilla, a pappe
hemplata, schuldyr bone
dorsus, tergus, tergum, bakke
spina, bakkbone
latus, syde
costa, rybbe
lumbus, the reynys [kidneys]
nates, butokkis
piga, a balokke
pellis, pellicula, cutis, skynne
cor, harte
venter, ventriculus, alnus, vterus, bely
vmbelicus, navyll
cor, corculum, herte [repeated]
pulmo, longys
diafragma, the myddryffe
iecur, mawe [belly; *jecur*, liver; several of these anatomical entries are confused]
epar, lyvyr
splen, mylt
lien, longutt [*lien*, milt, or spleen]
intestinum, a bowelle [after *a*, *gu*- deleted; beginning of gutte?]

Folio 294b

extum, precordium, viscuseris, the inwarde [*viscuseris*, error for *visceris*]
podex, lingeo, anarse hole [*anarse*, written as one word]
ren, kydney
pinguedo, adeps, armua, fatte
fluxus, lienteria, the flix [flux]
crus, femur, a thy
genu, a kne
poples, poplex, a hamme
anca, an ankley [not in *MED*; *OED* labels as *dial.*]
tibea, legge
cauilla, spelebone [*OED*, *speel-bone*, small bone of leg or arm]
sura, schynne
musculus, brawne of the legge [added in a later hand]
internodium, knebone
pes, vestigium, fote
coxa, an ankley [repeated; *coxa*, hip]
talus, calx, calcaneus, hele
planta, plantula, scrutum, subtile, a plante [sole of foot]
callus, duricias, the hard of the fo[te]
allux, articulus, a too
gressus [glossed on next leaf]

Folio 295a

incessus, passus, progressus, progressio, perfectus, perfectio, a goyng
regressus, regressio, reuersio, redditus, a turnyng agayne

aduentus, ascensus, discensus, commyng too
discessus, recessio, resesus, a departyng
gustus, tastyng
odoratus, smellyng
auditus, heryng
visus, visio, a syȝthe
tactus, towchyng

De Vestibus
[Clothes]

vestis, vestimentum, vestitus, inutatorium, indumentum, ranla, regulum, ray [array; possibly *OED*, *ray*, sb.[4], striped cloth]
vestis poliunita, multicolor, myllyd [error for *medle*: *MED*, n. (a), 2. (a), cloth made of wools dyed and mingled before being spun]
pannus [not glossed]
lanugo, lana, wolle
camisia, interula, subicula, a shert
bracco, femorale [not glossed]

Folio 295b

tribiaca, a strapyll [*OED*, *strapple*, covering for lower body, with a band laced round; *tribiaca*, *tribrica*, breeches]
lumbare, renale, braccala, a breygyrdyll [*MED*, *brei-girdel*, var. of *brech-girdel*, loincloth; see fol. 317a]
laterale, perizona, corsett
tunica, kyrtyll
supertunica, surcotte
collobium, taberdum, tabarde
toga, epitogium, gowne
calumus, cloca, clauus, armulansa, cloke
mantellus, clauus, palla, pallium, lena, aclas, mantell
teristrum, superus, supera, institа, sagana, rochett [smock, frock, cloak, or mantle]
collarium, collaria, a colar
manica, sleve
lacuna, gore
manicipium, a spayer [*OED*, *spare*, sb.[2], slit in robe or gown]
fibula, button
sutura, consutura, seme
ora, fimbria, hemme
limbus, burdowre [border]
seruigulum, zona, baltheus, stropheus, gyrdyll

Folio 296a

ceanicmitum, textum, saynt [ceint, belt]
bucula, bokyll
lingula, tonge [*OED*, 14. a., pin of a buckle or brooch]
stipa, stothe [*OED*, *stooth*, stud]
pendulum, mordaculum, pendant
transunarium, sparbelett [not in *OED*; perhaps a device to close the *spayer*, above]
bursa, loculus, marcipium, purse
culter, cultellus, cimpulus, artavus, knyfe [*cimpulus*, *simpulus*, ladle]
acumen, acies, an egge [edge]
manubrium, manutentum, hafte
sindula, blade
spera, sperula, a verelle [ferrule (?)]
senaculum, spirasinus, tonge [*OED*, 14. m., part of knife-blade fixed in haft; first cit., 1853]
vagina, schethe
capicium, hode
tena, howse [error for *howve*, hood; *tena*, *t(a)enia*, headband]
pilius, cappe
flameum, flameolum, kerchyffe
multiplicium [not glossed]
sudarium, micarium, sudary [sweat cloth]
trica, tricatura, tressowre [*tressure*, woman's headband]

peplum, wympyll
reticulum, calle [*caul,* woman's cap]
victa, vinculum, redunculum, bonde

Folio 296b

[?]ita, idem [also glosses *bonde*]
inuolutorium, salamandrum, talamacus, volopere [*voluper,* cap]
coronale, crinale, coronall
speculum, mirowre
petten, coma, combe
crispatorium, calanustrum, est instrumentum crispandi crines [not glossed; Lat. = curling iron]
anulus, anula, ryng
monde, firmaculum, spinterulum, spinter, mus, murenula, torques, an owche [*MED, nouch,* gem, brooch, etc.]
mauris, anulus maure, armilla, ornatus humeri [not glossed *maure,* Moorish; *ornatus humeri,* bracelets]
perachillides, ornatus brachij [not glossed; bracelets]
ciroteca, glove
manca, mancus, mita, mitayne
cirotecarius, glover
caliga, hose
legula, a leyner [*MED, lainer,* lace, thong, strap]
subligare, gartar
sotular, calceus, calciamentum, schoo
solea, suppedia, sole
laqueus, cenea, lace

Folio 297a

pedana, subpedana, wampay [*OED, vamp,* sock; records sp. *wampe*; *vamp,* also part of shoe or boot]
calipodium, pateyne [*patten,* shoe, sometimes with thick sole to increase stature]
liguipes, sorripedium, stylt

De Ecclesia et Sibi Pertinentis
[Concerning the Church
and its appurtenances]

ecclesia, templum, monasterium, prophanum, dolobrum, basilica, archisterium, azilum, chyrche
oratorium, chapell
capella, idem [also glosses preceding entry]
basis, columna, pylar
fundamentum, grownde
eristilium, chapterhowse [*eristelium* = *peri-*]
capitulum, idem [also glosses preceding entry]
arculus, arcus, semarculus, arche
volta, testudo, woute [vault]
selateira, tecaria, selowre [cellar]
postis, post
trabes, beme
trabecla, idem est [also glosses preceding entry]
laquiare, laquiarium, brace
tegimen, tegimellum, superrcopyll [not in *OED*; *MED, couple,* 3., one of a pair of rafters]
festum, raftyr
fastegium, doma, tectura, roffe [roof]

Folio 297b

tegula, later, tyle
tegularius, tector, tylar
paris, murus, menia, maceries, walle
stillicidium, guttarium, aquilicium, guttyr
fenestra, fenestrale, wyndow
ristus, fenestrale, fenestrall [windowpane]
vitrum, vitriolum, saphirus,

glasse
ara, altare, autyr
superalta vel superaltere [not glossed]
imago, statua, species, figura, ymage
frontale, tabula, frontelle [*MED, frountel,* decorative hanging for altar]
lintheus, lintheamen, tualla, manitergium, towelle
corpera, a corperace [*MED, corperas,* altar cloth]
calix, chalesse
patena, patenne [paten, plate used for bread in the Eucharist]
viola, cruett [cruet, small vessel for sacramental wine]
lauatorium, lauatory
sacrarium, sakyrryng [*OED, sacring,* 1. b., the consecrated elements]
pixis, boxe
hostia, oblata, viaticum, the sacrament

Folio 298a

eucaristia, idem [glosses preceding line]
missa, a masse
missale, missalle
euangelia, gospeller
euangelium, gospelle
epistola, pystyll
epistolarium, pystyll boke
sacerdos, capellanus, sacrista, flamen, presbiter, preste
diaconus, euangelista, leuita, decen
subdiaconus, subdiaconies, subdekyn
epistolista, pistiller
exorcista, lectora, colett [acolyte; *MED* lists sp. *accolett, colet*]
acolitus, idem [glosses preceding entry]
lexionarium, legenda, legentt [book of saints' legends; *MED* lists sp. *legent, legant*]
superpellicium, surplesse
rochitum, rochet [smock, frock, cloak, or mantle; here a vestment worn by a bishop or abbot]
talaris, alba, albe
tunicale, dalmatica, tunakyll
insula, casula, chesabyll
planeta [not glossed; *OED, planet,* sb.[2], chasuble; first cit., 1602]
bissus, whyȝt sylke
purpura, purpull
sericum, sylke
coccus, coccinium, red sylke
perura, perure, sorago, limbus, hemlyste [*MED, liste,* n. (2), border, edge, hem]

Folio 298b

capa, cope
thuribulum, incensatorium, censer
turribularius, incensator, a censear [not in *MED*; censer bearer]
nauicula, aceria, schyppe [incense boat]
thus, incensum, tumana, encens
serrus, cereolus, serge [*OED, serge,* 1. b., curtain; only cit. from Wycliffe]
torta, tortula, tosta, tostelle, torticium, torche
cera, wexe
candala, candyll
lampas, lampe
[At top of column 2, illegible line added in later hand]
papirus, arpus, rysche [*OED, rush,* 1. b., rush light]
lichinus, famale, weke [wick; *lichinus,* perhaps error for *lechythus,* oil flask]
sizendula [not glossed; perhaps = wick trimmer (*cis-*)]
lanterna, lucerna, lanterne

cucubrum, crucibolum, cressett
candelabrum, candelaforium, candylstykke
absconsa, sconse
crux, crucula, crosse
crucifixus, crucifix
signum, vexillum, baner
aspersorium, strenkyll [*OED*, *strinkle*, holy-water sprinkler]
isopus, paxilla, paxe [osculatory; image of Crucifixion to be kissed; *isopus*, *hyssopus*, holy-water sprinkler; belongs with preceding entry]

Folio 299a

amphora, aquarium, halywatyrfatt [*-fatt*, vat]
processionale, processionarium, processionall
vespere, vesperi, euynsonge
completorium, complynne
matutine, mateynys
cancellusa, chanselle
chorus, quyer
lectrinum, pulpitum, ambo, lettyrne [lectern; *MED* records sp. *letirn*]
stallum, ferculum, stalle
psalterium, sawter
psalmus, psalme
psalmodizacio, versikyll
ordinale, ordinalle
portiforium, portouse [*OED*, *portas*, portable breviary]
antiphona, anteme
troparium, tropar
antifonarium, antifonar
manuale, manualle [*manuale*, corr. from *-ulale*]
imnare, ymnarre [*MED*, *imnar*, hymnal]
precentor, cantor, chawntar
latania, precacio, rogacio, deprecacio, intercessio, interuentus, interuencio, precacio, precamen, prayr [*precacio* repeated]
Nomini et genus huius precis [not glossed; explains preceding series]

Folio 299b

Benefi[ci]um, benefactum, meritum, godedede
obsequium, deseruyng
officium, incroitus, an offyce [*incroitus*, error for *intr-*]
colecta, oracio, colett
gradale, gradarium, grayle [*MED*, *graiel*, gradual]
gradus, grece [*MED*, *gre*, n. (1), one of the gradual Psalms; *grece* (*grese*, not in *MED*), a collection of these]
tractus, trakke [tract]
sequencia, sequens
offertorium, offerenda, offertory
prefacio, preface
comino, comyn [perhaps *MED commune*, 3. (e), *commune belle* (shared by members of the community)]
postcomino, a postcomyn [postcommon, prayer after mass; *postcomino*, *postcommunio*]
flagellum, a vischar [*whisk(er)*, for flies; not in *OED*, s.v. *f-*, *v-*, *w-*; *flagellum*, whisk for protecting the Host]
flabellum idem est [glosses preceding entry]
messefugium [glosses preceding entry; *messefugium*, error for *musca-*? fly whisk]
sacrista, sexten
sacristaria, sacristar
vestibulum, vestry
vestimentum, vestiment [OED records sp. *veste-*]
ornamentum, ornament
tintinnabulum, sakyrryngbell[e] [sacring bell, rung at elevation of Host]
campanilla [glosses preceding entry]
nola, kocbelle [*MED*, *coke-belle*,

small bell]
bactillus, clapyr [*bactillus,* perhaps *bacci-*; but see fol. 319a]
pulsatorium, classicum, a pele [peal]
corda,cordula, rope
restis, resticula, funis, corde

Folio 300a

funiculus, idem [glosses preceding entry]
rudens, autempna, cabylle
campanile, campanarium, classatorium, belhowse
tolus, sumuntas, toppe [top (of a roof?); *tolus,* pommel of sword or knife, from Gk. *tholos,* domed edifice]
ventilocrium, cheruca, wedyrkoc [weathercock]
porticus, porche
ianua, porta, valua, fores, bifores, a ȝate
cardo, herre [*MED, herre,* hinge]
superluminare, ouyrleyse [not in *MED, OED*; however, *OED, lace,* 4., tie-beam; *superluminare* = lintel]
serra, serula, lokke
pessulum, lacche
repagulum, idem [glosses preceding entry]
obex, clatrus, vectis, barre
anulus, pulsatorium, ryng [recognizes the pun: jewel, sound of a bell]
aditus, introitus, ingressus, an enterryng
exitus, regressus, regressio, an owtepassyng
portitor, ianitor, portar

Folio 300b

hostiarius, an huscher [usher]
portula, posticus, posticum, posterula, posterne
fons, baptisterium, fonte
baptismus, crystyn dome
ba[p]tisma, offium baptismi [not glossed; *offium,* error for *-cium*]
crismale, a crysome [chrism]
crismatorium, a crismatory
crisma, creme
gerris, craticulacinerferrum, lattis of yrun
cathecuminus est ille qui quisquem ad fidem catholicam et non prius baptisus [not glossed]
neophitus, idem [not glossed]
credulitas, fides, beleve
spes, speraco, hope [*speraco,* error for *-cio*]
cimitorium, atrium, poliandrum, inhumatorium, a chyrche ȝarde
clausura, clausum, septum, a close
interclausura, intersticium, sperrentyr close [not in *OED*; perhaps from *spar,* sb.[1], 3. a., bar of wood to fasten gate or door]
craticula, craticularium, cratis, a grede[y]run [gridiron]
sepulcrum, monumentum, a graue [continued on next leaf]

Folio 301a

sercofagum, bustum, mausoleum, theoremna, tumulus, tumba, fossa, a graue
feretrum, loculus, libitina, a bere [bier; see fol. 14a]
reliquie, relikis
exinie, induuie [glosses preceding entry]
cadauer, carene [carrion, corpse]
exsequie, funus sunt exsequia mortuoris [not glossed]
testamentum, testament [will]
executor, an executor
particom, a dole [*MED, dolen,* v. (2), distribute alms; *particom,* error for *-cium*]
distribucio, diuisio, a dole [contin-

ues preceding entry]
elemosina, roga, an almis
elimosinarius, an amner [almoner; perhaps should be transcribed *aumner*]
partitor, distributor, a deler [*MED, deler,* (b), one who gives alms]
memoria, commemoracio, a mynd
obliuio, minoria, a forgetyng
scala, scaruale, ascensus, ascensio, laddyr [*scaruale,* error for *scal-*?]
discensus, discensio, a goyng downe

Nomina Prelatorum Ecclesie
[Names of prelates of the Church]

papa, pope
cardinalis, cardinalle

Folio 301b

patriarcha, patriarke
archiepiscopus, primas, an arse buschoppe [*arse,* common substitution for *arch-*; see *OED, archbishop*]
episcopus, presul, autistes, pontifex, buschoppe
prelatus, prelate
mitra, mityr
baculus, pedum, cambuca, a crose [crozier]
cruciarius, cambucarius, a crosyer [crozier bearer]
decanus, dene
archidiaconus, an arse decon [see *arse buschoppe* above]
canonis regularis siue secularis, canon
prebendarius, prebendar
rector, a persone [parson]
vicarius, a vycary [*OED* records sp. fourteenth-sixteenth century]
papatus, primatus, archiepiscopatus, episcopatus, deconatus, archidiaconatus, canonicatus, prebenda, rectoria, vicaria, sunt nomina dignitatum et officiarum predictorum [not glossed]
abbas, an abbott
abbathia, an abbey
abbatissa [not glossed]
prior, prior
priorissa, pryoresse
religiosis, a religiose
religio, a religioun

Folio 302a

regula, a rule
ordo, an ordyr
monachus, munke
monacha, monialis, nonne
abitus, an abytt [habit]
velum, wayle [veil]
cucullus, cowle
claustrum, cloyster
dormitorium, dortyr
sonnus, sopor, soporacio, dormicio, dormitacio, a slepe
somnium, dreme
refectorium, frayter
capitulum, chapter
caplium, constry [consistory; *MED* records sp. *constri*]
consistorium idem est [not glossed]
officialis, an offichall
officialitas, officium eius [not glossed]
commissarius, commissary
commissio, potestas eius [not glossed]
aperitor, a somnar [summoner]
registrum, register
registrator, custos eius eiusdem [not glossed]
procorator, procture
procuracio, procuracy
aduocatus, a vocatt [advocate]
causedicus, orator
causa, occasio, pretextus, no-

men, res, an enchesone [cause, reason]
iudex, a iugge [judge; continued on next leaf]

Folio 303b

arbiter, sensor, a iugge
iudicium, sentencia, examen, arbitrium, sensura, a dome [judgment]
mediator, sequester, caducator, a mediator
scola [not glossed]
gignasium [not glossed]
studium, stody
vel applicacio mentis ad aliquid agentum [interlinear; not glossed]
magister, monitor, doctor, scriba, doctrinator, a master [continued in next column]
instructor, informator, precepter, didaculus, petagogus, autor, vicedoctor, vicemonitor, submonitor, a master
hostiarius, an huscher [usher]
segista, sedista, a segister [not in *OED*; perhaps = *sexton,* for which *OED* records somewhat similar spellings; the meaning of the Lat. cannot be ascertained]
doctrina, doctrinacio, dogma, documentum, instruccio, informacio, erudicio, a techyng

Folio 304a

palnutorium idem est [glosses preceding entry]
materia, materies, theme, a matter
dictamen, dictacio, carmen, poema, a dytyng [glosses preceding entry; composing (in writing); the scribe associates writing, poetry, prophecy, and witchcraft]
dictator, poeta, vates, a dytor [*MED, ditour,* author, writer, orator, scribe]
propheta, persagus, divinator, sortilagus, magus, incantator, carminator, vates, a prophet
aruspex, mathematicus, augur, ariolus, a wyche
sortilegium, incantacio, mathetis, augurium, a wychecrafte
sors, fortuna, casus, occasio, successus, euentus, fatam, omen, a happe [fate]
infortunium, euyll happe

Folio 302b

[Misbound; preceded by fols. 303b, 304a]
solacium, sport or play
recracio [glosses preceding entry; error for *-eacio*]
littera, grama, letter [altered from *gr-*]
scriptura, grafium, exoraco, protraccon, a wrytyng [*exoraco,* error for *-cio*]
grammatica, diolectica, retorica, arsmetrica, astronomia, geometria, sunt septem artes liberales et inde descendunt grammaticus, dialeticus, retoricus, arsmetricus, musicus, geometricus, astronomus, et astrologus [not glossed]
ars, artificium, sciencia, crafte or conyng
artifex, operarius, operator, operarius, a craftyman, warkeman [repeated]
iurista, legista, legister [lawyer]
canonista, legista, canonister [expert in canon law]
ius, lex, lawe
iuscionnen, iuscitule, de auctate dicitur teologia diuinite [not glossed; *auctate,* error for *-oritate*]
theologus, artifer, dyvyner [theologian]

Folio 303a

iussum, iussio, imperium, admonicio, preceptum, precipico, spacio, a commandyng [*precipico*, error for *-icio*]
discipulus, condiscipulus, a dyscipulle
disciplina, disciplinacio, a lernyng
clericus, clericulus, clerke
clerimonia, clergy
clerus, congregacio clericorum videlicit prelatorum [not glossed]
liber, libellus, pagina, a boke
volumen, codex, codicellus [glosses preceding entry]
librius, custos librorum [not glossed]
librarium, scrutor librorum [not glossed]
almarium, armariolum, libriteca, biblioteca, repositorium, an almarye [*MED*, *almerie*, place for storing or safekeeping]
biblia, biblioteca, a bybyll [*biblioteca* repeated in error]
mergo, a mergyn
linea, a lyne
interlinium, an enterlyne
glosa, a glose [gloss]
glosator, interliniator, a gloser
pennare, pennarium, a penarre [*OED*, *penner*, case for pens]

Folio 305b

[Misbound; this folio begins a series of folios bound out of order]
penna, calamus, a pen
cornu, a horne [inkhorn]
encaustum, atrrimentum, sepia, ynke
tabula, tabella, diptica, tabyllys [writing tablet (folding, as *diptica* suggests)]
stilus, grafium, a poyntell [*OED*, *pointel*, stylus]
pugillar vel pugillaris penna vel corim vel tabula manualis [not glossed]
diligencia, cura, curiositas, assiduitas, opera, solicitudo, besynesse [diligence]
negligencia, pigricia, torpor, torpedo, desidia, ignauia, slowythe or necligens [*slowythe*, sloth]
malefactum, maleficium, demeritu, a mysdede
castigacio, correctio, correptio, a chastyng [*MED*, *chasting*, chastising]
virga, virgula, flagellum, a rode [rod, whip]
ferula, percussorium, a palmer [not in *MED*; *OED*, *palmer*, sb.^{3} flat piece of wood used for striking the palm of the hand; here, however, the word signifies the blow itself]; see *pedus*, fol. 162b.

Folio 306a

suburbum, perastiuum, subbarbys [suburbs]
sambucus, eldyr tre [*eldyr*, altered from *alder*]
loripes, extales [not glossed; *loripes* refers to the clumsy-footed and to the rectum]
gnafus, duarfe
semotus, postpositus, sepositus, remotus, leyd a parte or remevyd
curio, a man of cowrte
lunaticus, limphaticus, a fransy man [*fransy*, *MED*, *frensie*, as noun only]
lippus, bleryed [blear-eyed]
strabo, a goglyyd [goggle-eyed]
calculus, calculosus, a man þat haue þe stone [kidney stone]
millus, mullus, mulleus, for a doggis coler

Folio 304b

mauistas, a thrush
tordus idem [glosses preceding entry]
coturnix, quayyll
mergus, a dydappyr [*MED*, *dive-dap*, a diving bird; sp. incl. *didopper*]
aspergo, cormaund [cormorant; *MED* does not include this sp.]
picus, bosard
capus, muscatte [*MED*, *muskete*, sparrow-hawk]
campestris, fyldfare
ergonia, schoueler [*OED*, *shovelard*, spoonbill; this sp. not recorded]
cardnell, goldfynche
ciuolus, chebell [*MED*, *chibol*, spring-onion]
epicaustorium, wrytyng chere [writing chair]
doca, polax
pupila, welke [not in *OED*; *pupil(la)*, disease of falcons; perhaps = *whelk*,[2] pustule]
asser, borde
directus, dismollday [*MED*, *dismal dai*, one of two days each month which were considered unlucky]
armilausa, cloke
lacinea, gore
multicum, rochett [smock, frock, cloak, or mantle]
alacrimonia, glaues [not in *MED*; perhaps *gloves*]
canistrum, paynyer [pannier, basket]
epilocarium, schelfe
plecta, matte
pedoforus, crosyer [*MED*, *crocer*, prelate's crozier-bearer]

Folio 305a

copia, abundancia, fertilitas, feracitas, ecuberancia, plentyvsnesse [altered (illegible)]
ferax, fertilis, copius, plenty
ecuberancia non est vestulencia, plenty ys no denty [*OED*, *dainty*, 5., anything estimable; cites Heywood's *Proverbs* (1562), "Plenty is no dainty"; also Tilley, P 425]
de malo in penis, þe lenger þe wors [evidently "concerning evil in afflictions"; however, there may be a mildly obscene joke: "concerning pain in the penis, the longer the worse"]
forum, forus, mercatum, merkytt
nundine, feyre
locus, vicus, stede [place (n.)]
verber, a long rod or a strype [blow with a whip]

Folio 306b

orbusis, blynde or be mome [be mum, be deprived of speech]
siromellum, wort [*ciromelum*, wort, grout for ale making]
trilicium, kersey [coarse woolen cloth]
corditectum, stomacher
pelta, scutum, bokeler [buckler]
epuglotum, þe throte bolle [throat boll, larynx]
rinda, a penent of a gyrdyll [pendant, part left hanging when girdle is tied]
cantabrum, horse brede [*MED*, *hors*, 8, *hors bred*, bread for horses, made of bean meal]
mamilia [not glossed]
malumgranatum, a pounde garned [pomegranate]
malum punicum idem est [glosses preceding entry]
pomum citriuum, oryng
prunum damscenum, damasyn
ordo subdiaconatus, subdekynry
diaconatus, dekynry
archidiaconatus, archedekynry
episcopatus, presulatus, byschyppery
ad ecclesiam sancte marie mat-

folon, whyt chapell
ecclesia sancti benedicti, besynk [not identified]

Folio 307a

acurrarium, a naglet [an aglet; *MED, aglet,* metal point at end of cord or ribbon]
angarius, keche poll [*MED, cacche-pol,* petty bailiff; two false starts, deleted]
cliens, sariant
pannitonsor, shereman [shearman, one who shears woolen cloth]
tiriaca, triakyll [treacle; medicinal compound, orig. a salve]
precentor, trebyll [treble (voice)]
intercentor, mene [mean, alto]
succentor, tenor
clarigator, haraud of armys
agilis, nemmell [nimble]
ledo, wreke of þe see [wreck (wrack) of the sea]
fusilla, custale [not glossed]
camberium, hempe sede
linarium, lynne sede
gagas, iete [jet (mineral)]
ibiscus, mistellyyne [mistletoe (?); *MED*; *mistiltine*; maslin, mixed grain (?); *OED* records sp. similar to, though not identical with, *mistellyyne*; *ibiscus* = marshmallow]
pignosus, dager full [not in *MED*; *pignosus,* refers to pledge, something pawned]
fungus, nostryngis [not in *OED, MED*; nose strings (?); a kind of mushroom?]
pomarium, orcherd
pomerium, hord of apyllys
ambria, ambyr
lambria, lamber [*MED, laumbre,* amber]
corallus, corall
mortuarium, cors present [not in *MED*; *OED, corse-present,* gift to clergy at a funeral; see Lindsay, *Ane Satire of the Three Estates,* line 1962]
fyltrum, stilarium [not glossed]

Folio 307b

plumacium, fedder bedde
reclinatorium, pelow
multrum, multrale, mylkyng payle
merga, pyke forke
assecretis, chamberlayn
aresponsis, stevard
torta, cake
sectio, swathe
filitura, spynnyng
valec [not glossed]
cerusa, a gode [good; see fol. 17a, where it is glossed *gerusa*]
feratorium, a plumell [not in *OED*; *pharetra,* quiver (for arrows)]
subtela [not glossed]
postela, cropyn [*MED, crouper, crupper*; this sp. not recorded]
ligo, pekese [pickax]
stansile, strepa, styrope [stirrup]
sarculum, wedyng hoke [weeding hook]
vncula vel plutulum, bokell
aurifrigium, gold wyer [gold wire; *aurifrigium,* orphrey, gold embroidery]
serum, wheyy

Folio 308a

uirgilium, demolitorium [not glossed]
stamen, werppe [warp (in weaving)]
licinatorium, slyke stone [*OED, sleekstone,* used for smoothing and polishing cloth]
pensum, yerne
maceries, a stone wall
marigo, stoc [*OED, stock,* 17., frame for spinning-wheel (?)]
spongea, sponge
spongio, to sponge

fuciludium, a carde [*MED*, *card*, n. (1), toothed comb for carding wool]
intero, to bred in a dysche [perhaps *breden*, roast, broil]
lura, moweth of a botell
saltus, lawne in a parke
pes meus somdolet, my fote slepyth [*somdolet*, error for *somno-*; the Lat. actually follows the Eng.; the scribe may be describing his current sensation]
auris mea formicat, tyn [not in *OED*; *auris mea formicat*, the ear rings or itches (as if crawling with ants)]
tinus, a whyte þorne
prinus, a blacke þorne
plumludium, a cokystell [not in *MED*; = cock's tail, some sort of plant]
floctus, a loke of wolle
villus [not glossed]
succosso, to trotte
ambulo, ambyll
impectoro, to take to herte
institutum, decretum, a ordinans
fassiculus, a botell of hey [bundle of hay]
orca, orcula, tankard
frigella, rodoke [ruddock, robin redbreast]
ornix, castriuergus, woodoke [woodcock; *OED* does not record this sp.]

Folio 308b

Nomina Villarum
[Names of Cities]

amiee, amyas
aurelianus, orlians
dublinea, dulyn [Dublin]
verlamecestria, villa sancti albani [not glossed; Saint Alban's]
gloucestria, glouerina, glocester
varwicus, warwyke
batonia, bath
ibernia, yrlond
brytannia, brytan
burgundia, burgundy
scocia, scotland
cornubia, cornwale
athene, atenys
vallia, walis
cancia, kente
sarisbira vel sarum, salysbery
eboracus, yorke
sandwycus, sandwyche
doveria, dover
vernona, vernone
elia, ely
linepiscopi, lynn
iudea, iury [Jewry]
wigornia, wurceter
wyntonia, wynchester
gasconia, gaskyn
lumbardia, lumbardy
septrina, shaftebery
licestria, leycester
ecexa, esexe
susexia, sussex
medylsexia, medylsex
norfolchia, nore fokke [altered from *norf-*]
northa [not glossed]
mediolanus, melyn [Melton? Middleton? Mediolanum was the Lat. name of Milan, though this city seems out of place here]
meldunus, malmysbery
burgus sancti petri, petyr borow
burgus sancti edmundi, saynt edmundis borow
iuo, sayt yue [*sayt*, error for *saynt*]
neotus, saynt nede
burgus santi albani, saynt albanys

Folio 309a

Hic incipit nominale sub compendio compilatus tam de fixis quam de mobilibus primu de vocabulis ad singula membra corporis humani spectantibus

[Here begins the *nominale*, including both animate and inanimate (concepts) and beginning with words for parts of the human body]
caput, hede
cinciput, the forparte of the hede
occiput, the nodyll
interciput, media pars [not glossed]
frontispicium, a toppe
vertex, hatrell [back of the head]
discrimen, the schade of the here [part of the hair]
crinis, a here
capillus, coma, pilus, a here
cerebrum, the brayne
cranium, the braynepanne
facies, faciecula, a face
tempus, tempyll
macula, spotte
papula, a blayne [*MED*, *bleine*, inflammatory swelling]
maxilla, gena, mala, faux, cheke
frons, forhede
cilium, browe
supercilium, the brow
intercilium id est spacium inter cilia [not glossed]
oculus, talmus, an ye
palpebra, the ye lyde
pupilla, the appyll of the ye
albucies, albugo, albinus, the whyte of the ye
acies, the syȝthe of the ye
nasus, a nose
naris, nostrell
intersinuum, the bryge of þe nose [*bryge*, altered from *brynge*]
purila, the poynt of þe nose
cartilago, the grystyll
rostrum, a byll
oirrus, a hobyll of bone [not in *MED*; error for *hok-*? *OED*, *huckle-bone*, hip or haunch bone; first cit., 1529]
polipus, the fylthe of the nose
salma, sputum, spetyll
orexis, dravelyng [*MED*, *dreveling*, slavering]
glabra, a scalle [*OED*, *scall*, skin disease]
mentum, chynne
molaris, grete tothe
os, mowthe
gene, bucca, cheke
lingua, glossa, tonge

Folio 309b

labrum, labium, lyppe
dens, tothe
penna, a penne
pluma, fedyr
plumatus, fedyrde
auris, auricula, ere
mandubila, maxilla, cheke bone
porrigo, a pokke
veruca, a werte
postula, a blayne [see fol. 309a]
vlcus, a byle [*MED*, *bile*, n. (2), ulcer]
gibbus, a bunche [hump]
giberber, struma, a byl be fore [swelling in front (as contrasted with hump)]
collum, nekke
guttur, gugurbium, throte
frontinella, nekke pytt
frumen, summa, ructa, rumen, pars gutturis [not glossed]
ysophagus, wesant [windpipe]
epiglotum, throte boll [throat boll, larynx]
ruga, reboll [not in *OED*; *ruga*, wrinkle; perhaps var. of *ripple*]
brachium, arme
stomachus, stomake
acelle, arme hole
ala, wyng
manus, hande
digitus, fyngyr
palma, nola, palme of the hande
pollex, thombe
index, schweyng fyngyr
medius, medyll fyngyr

medicus, leche fyngyr ["physican" finger, perhaps because he used it in examination]
auriculus, lytyll fyngyr ["ear" finger, used to clean the ear]
pugnus, fyste
vnguis, vngula, nayle
iuctura, ioynte
corpus, body
cutis, pellis, skynne
tergum, dorsum, bakke
spondile, bakke bone
venter, alnus, vterus, bely
vmbelicus, navyll
natis, a buttoke
cauda, tayle [*cauda*, altered from *-am*]
dica idem est [*dica*, tally; ME *tayle* represents both tally and tail, as the conclusion of Chaucer's *Shipman's Tale* shows]
lumbus, rayne [kidney]
thorax, brystbone

Folio 310a

vber, mamma, a pappe
pectus, breste
latus, syde
costa, rybbe
pubes, a schare [*OED*, *share*, sb.^{2}, division or fork of the body; pubic region or groin]
femur, crus, a thy
veretrum, putibunda, a pyntyll [penis]
testiculus, genitale, a balloke
piga, a ballokkod [scrotum]
anus, cullus, an ars
squama, a scale [(fish) scale; perhaps also a skin disease]
poples, a hamme
matrix est pellis in qua concipitur infans; stera idem est [not glossed]
viscus, intestinum, extum, a bowell
scrutum, a trype
diafragma, a mydrefe
pulpa, the brawnde [*MED*, *braun*, muscular part, this sp. not recorded]
epar, lyvyr
splen, mylte
cor, herte
pulmo, longe
lecur, mawe [belly, stomach; *lecur*, perhaps error for *je-*, *iecur*, liver; see fol. 294a]
ren, kydney
cadauer, carene [carrion, corpse]
burbulum, nowblys [*MED*, *noumbles*, edible viscera; records *noubles* as a sp. error]
cepum, talow
obdomen, grese
pinguedo, adeps, fattnesse
sanguis, cruor, blode
omestra, mygreme [*MED*, *migraine*, headache; records sp. *migreme*]
fel, galle
prina, flygge [*MED*, *flegge*, reed or rush (?); Lat. adds *penna volat, prima* (error for *prina*) *natat, supprina vacillat*. A reed could be thought to "swim"]
stercus, a torde
merda, a turdyll [small turd; *OED* records only *treddle*, sheep dung]
merdula, parua merda [not glossed]
zirbus, a gutte
genu, knee
tibea, legge
internodium, kne bone
sura, schynne
linus, neruus, synow
vena, a weyne
os, bone

Folio 310b

medulla, mary [*marrow*; *MED* records sp. *mari*]
canulla, pynne bone [*OED*, *pin*, 6.,

projecting bone of the hip; first cit., 1703; *canulla*, perhaps confused with *cauilla*, ankle]
patula, a pynne
fragus, wryste
pes, fote
apostema, a postome [*MED*, *apostem*, abscess; this the aphetic form]
vertebra, whyrleborne [error for *-bone*]
sinus, a bosome
grabatum, gremium, a lappe
musculus, the calfe of the legge
callus, planta, the sole of the fote
talus, hele
allux, grete tooe [altered from *th-*]
articulus, lytyll too
vulnus, wonde
crista, cokkiscombe
iuba, a mane
sudor, swetyng
lacrima, tere
scabies, a scabbe
corona, crowne
vesica, bladyr
tuber, a tod stole

Nomina diuersoris hominum
[Names of various men]

imparator, emperowre
rex, regulus, kyng
princeps, prynce
dux, duke
dominus, lorde
comes, erle
vicicomes, a schreve
baronis, erle
miles, knyȝthe
armiger, squer
iudex, iusticiarius, iuge
burgencis, burgesse
libertinus, franklyn
ciues, citezyn
heres, an eyr [heir]
thesaurarius, threserer [treasurer]
maior, a meyr
apostulus, a postyll [apostle]
herimita, an erimytt
propheta, a profett
preco, a bedyll
senescallus, a stuvarde
marischallus, marchalle
hospitularius, hospituler
balliuus, bayly
nuncius, messenger
cursor, currur [courier]
papa, pope
patriarcha, patriarke
cardinalis, a carnalle [*MED* does not include this sp., *OED* lists *carnal*, sb.[2], as a perversion of cardinal, first cit., 1528]

Folio 311a

archipiscopus, arche bisschoppe
episcopus, bysschoppe
archidiaconus, arche decon
decanus, a dene
cancellarius, chansellar
suffraganius, a suffrigane
abbas, abbotte
prior, a prior
supprior, suppriur
monachus, monke
canonicus, chanon
celerarius, a celerarius, a celerar
sacrista, sexten
notarius, notarye
officialis, an officialle
presbiter, sacerdos, flamen, capellanus, a preste
comissarius, a commissarye
rector, a persone [parson]
frater, brothyr
doctor, techer
diaconus, leuita, deken
subdiaconus, subdekon
causidicus, a pleter [pleader (at court)]
magister, monitor, petagogus, instructor, summonitor, a master
accolitus, a colett [*MED*, *colite*,

acolyte; also records sp. *colet*]
exsorcista, lector, ianitor, a benett [*MED*, *benet*, one of the minor orders of secular clergy, the order of exorcists]
clericus, clerke
compatriata, contryman [fellow countryman]
poeta, poete
romanus, romayne
iudeus, a iue [Jew]
sarazenus, a sarsone [Saracen]
maritus, hosebonde
vir, man
homo, man
homunculus, homecellus, lytyl man [*homunculus*, altered from *homunsculus*]

Nomina officiorum
[Names of officials]

camerarius, chambyrly[n]
pantarius, panterer [*MED*, *paneter*, officer in charge of pantry; does not include this sp.]
pincerna, buttler
cocus, coke
archimarus, mastercoke
lixa, kychyn page
ianitor, portar
scolaris, scholar
seruus, seruante

Folio 311b

famulus, seruante
garcon, knave
sponsus, spowse
puer, chylde
latro, fur, thefe
predo, vespilis, clauiger, robber
primipilus media producta, vexillifer, baner berer

Nomina artificum
[Names of artisans]

emptor, byer
venditor, siller
membranarius, parchment maker
figulus, ollarius, potter
vrnarius, pycher maker
campanarius, bellmaker
apotecarius, spyser
clauicarius, key maker
iconomus, howsebonde [husbandman]
victor, an ouyr commer
riuolus, pedler
carpentarius, carpintar
pandoxator, bruer
scurra, a harlatt [knave, scoundrel]
piscator, fyscher
vrsarius, berewarde [bearward, keeper of bears]
fossor, dyker [ditcher]
plantator, setter [*OED*, *setter*, 2. a., one who sets stones or bricks in a building]
ortolanus, ortilio, gardiner
tector, thecher [thatcher]
anceps, fowler
auigerulus, pulter
tollenarius, toller [tax collector]
rusticus, villarius, fyldeman
messor, repar [reaper]
falcator, mower
instigator, fugator, auctor, dryver
scinarius, holder
auriga, bigarius, carter
forestarius, lucarius, siluarius, foster [forester]
pastor, herdeman
opilio, archimandrita, scheparde
vaccus, cowherde
equinarius, horsherde
molendinarius, myllner
azinarius, asse herde

Folio 312a

bubulcus, oxe herde
subbulcus, porcarius, swyne herde
enoycus, gote herde

ancarius, gose herde
pictor, peynter
scultor, grauer
cissor, tayler
smigmator, soper [soapmaker]
faber, smythe
faberculus, paruus faber [not glossed]
aurifaber, golde smythe
textor, wever
pugil, champion
mercator, merchawnte
mercenarius, mersor
pannarius, draper
pelliparius, skynner
latomus, cementarius, masone
barbitonsor, barber
hostiarius, vscher [usher]
architinens, sagittarius, archer
pugnator, fyȝter
capellarius, hatter
venator, honter
vestigator, tracer [tracker (here associated with the hunt); *OED*, first cit., 1552]
gemellus, vterinus, twyne
frunitor, tanner
hospiciarius, howsekeper [*MED*, *hous*, 7., *hous-keper*, overseer, steward]
sellarius, sadler
gladiator, furbur [*MED*, *fourbour*, smith who polishes metal]
lictor, tortor, tormentowre
discolus, trutannus, truant
allutarius, cordwenar [*MED*, *cordewaner*, one who makes shoes of cordovan leather]
sutor, sowter [maker or mender of shoes]
pictaciator, cobler
fullo, fuller [fuller (of cloth)]
alumptor, lymner [*MED*, *limnour*, illuminator of manuscripts]
ligator, bynder [*MED*, *binder*, (a), bookbinder]
baiulator, berer
arator, erer [plowman]
herpicator, harower
vascularius, turner [*OED*, *turner*, one who fashions objects from wood; but *vascularius*, worker in metal]
cipharius, copper [*MED*, *cupper*, cup maker]
zonarius, girdyller
cultellarius, cuttler
cirotecarius, glover
ferrarius, ferror [ferrier]
funditor, slyngar [*OED*, *slinger*, one who casts missiles by means of a sling; here perhaps sling maker]

Folio 312b

sumtarius, sumpter [driver of pack-horses]
carbonarius, colier
lorimarius, lorymere [*MED*, *lorimer*, worker in small ironware]
corbio, baskett maker
sanguinator, flecbotomator, blode letter
murator, warmaker [error for *wal-*, i.e., wallmaker]
epigmator, furbur [smith who polishes metal; *gladiator*, fol. 312a]
rotarius, wheler
casuarius, chesemonger
auxionarius, hucster
auxionatrix, muler [not in *OED*, *MED*; evidently a female huckster]
saparius, oynynseller [onion seller]
pomilio, costard mongar [apple seller]
tabernarius, caupo, tauerner
candelarius, chandler
cerarius, tapermaker
scriptor, wryter
archonista, bower [bow maker]
metellus, reue [*metellus*, altered from *-uns*]
nummilarius, monetarius, mony maker
inpendor, pyndor [*OED*, *pinder*, of-

ficer of a manor who pens up beasts]
agellarius, heywarde
legista, legistar [lawyer]
arcista, an arceder [*MED*, *arcister*, one who professes the liberal arts (though we question the word as an error); this sp. not recorded]
theologus [not glossed]
bacilarius, bachuler [*bachelor* (of arts)]
receptor, receyver [*OED* provides no special meanings]
mendicus, beggar
citherator, citharista, liricen, harper
buccinator, trumper
timpanizator, taberer
simphanizator, simphaner [player on the symphony, a word used vaguely for various stringed instruments]
sitolator, sitoler [player on the citole (stringed instrument)]
organista, orgonar
cinislenis, cenerarius, an ax blower [*ax*, error for *ash*; *cenerarius*, error for *cinerarius*, charcoal burner; *MED* has *assh-brennere*, maker of potash, but no *-blower*]
rumaticus, snyveler [*snyvel*, mucus; entry perhaps intended humorously]
momilarius, brechemake[r] [error for *broche-*; *momilarius*, error for *mon-*; see *broche*, fol. 319b]
anularius, ryng maker
vaginarius, schethemaker
cristator, tynker
nauta, schyppman
naucleris est ille qui regit nauem [not glossed]
pollitrudiator, bulter [bolter, sifter of grain]
pistor, baker

Nomina mulierum sunt recitanda
[Women's names are listed]

[Only two women's occupations are listed, which suggests that perhaps a folio has been lost, since this rubric occurs at the end of a folio; however, the list appears to be continued on fol. 320a.]
imperatrix [not glossed]
regina, qwene

Folio 313a

faretra, an arowgyrdyll [*MED*, *arwe*, 2., *-girdel*, girdle for holding arrows]
vanga, spade
denarius, peny
solidus, schelyng
marca, marke
libra, pownde
talentum, talent [coin, sum of money]

Nomina rerum pertinencia
pandoxatorio et pistrino
[Names of things pertaining to
the mill and the bakery]

pasta, dowe [dough]
farina, mele
polenta, similago, flowyr
furfur, bran
fermentum, sowyr dowe
fermentatus, sowyrde
rotabulum, moldyng borde
taretorium, sarge [*OED*, *searce*, sieve or strainer; *taretorum*, *tiratantrum*, bolting cloth; cf. *tarantarum* below]
pincella, pincela, brayke [*MED*, *brake*, pestle (no sp. in *-ay-*, *-ai-*)]
polentriduum, boltyng clothe
tarantarum, a temys [*OED*, *temse*, sieve]
cribrum, syfe [sieve]
alneus, trowght [*alneus*, perhaps *alu-*]
costa, rybbe [*OED* provides no special senses pertinent to baking, brewing]
focarium, herthe stone
flamicia, ignacia, torta, cake

libum, wastell [fine bread]
placenta, wygge [*placenta, placentula*, bun; perhaps a wedge-shaped cake]
artocopus, symnell [*OED, simnel*, bread made with fine flour]
grapha, wafyr
pastellus, pasty
pala, pele [*OED, peel*, sb², baker's shovel]
granomellum, ciromellum, worte [wort, grout for ale making; altered from *growte*]
attromellum, growte [see preceding entry; *attromellum*, perhaps error for *granomellum*]
area, flowyr [floor]
cupus, cupa, a fatt [vat]
modius, buschell
granata, mel
cernida, tappe
fex, draggis [dregs]
segisterium, draffe [*MED, draf*, 1. (a), chaff, husks]
situla, bukkett
celicium, heyr [*MED, here*, n. (2), covering originally made of goat's hair and used by seamen]
saccus, sakke
saculus, bagge
pomarium, orcharde
mel, hony
et inde melli[?] [interlinear; not glossed; continued on next leaf]

Folio 313b

mellatus, melifluus [not glossed]
fauus, hony kombe
cadus, barell
doleum, tonne [tun]
onoferum, costrell [*MED, costrel*, flask, bottle]
obba, botell
ciphus, kuppe
crater, patera, a pese [*OED, pece*, cup]
murra, maser
clipsidra, spigott
olla, fidelia, potte
vrna, pycher
vrnula, pynte
amphora, orca, tankarde
lagena, a golon [error for *galon*? *lagena*, flask, flagon]
laguncula, potellus, potell [*OED, pottle*, two quarts]
quarta, quarte
vinum, wyne
mustum, muste
sesara, sydyr
medo, methe [mead]
idromellum [not glossed]
claretum, clarett
ceruisia, selia, ale
piretum, perre [perry (juice of pears)]
nectar, pyment [spiced wine]
acetum, aycell [eisell, vinegar]

Nomina piscium et instrumentorum cum quibus capiuntur
[Names of fish and of the equipment with which they are caught]

murena, lamprey
salmo, samon
muremila, lamprey
alec, heryng
piscis, pisciculus [not glossed]
anguilla, an ele
ostrium, oyster
cancer, crabbe
lucius, luse [luce, pike]
magarius, makare[l]
polipus, lobstar
canis, dogfysche
cetus, whale
dentrix, pyke
pecten, playse
trude, troyde [trout]
morus, mewyke [not in *MED, OED*; *morus*, cod]

capito, bullhede [*MED, bole-hed,* mullet]

Folio 314a

genesta idem est [*genesta,* broom (plant); evidently the folio is misbound; see folio 321a]
arundo, canna, calamo, rede
seliqua, pescode
folliculus, a sluthe [*OED, slough,* 2. c., husk; first cit., 1660]
germen, burgenyng
semen, sede
manipulus, gelina, handful
garba, schefe
arconius, a reke [rick (of hay)]
fenum, hey
concelluna, stok of hey
gramen, grasse
herba, an erbe
omulus, acernus, hepe [*MED, hepe,* n. (2), (rose) hip]
secuta, hemloke
suna, crop of a tre [*MED, crop,* 2. (c), crown, top, or foliage of a tree]
rustus, groste [*MED, gorst,* gorse, metathesized]
olus, worte
magnuderis, cawlestokke [*MED, calstoke,* cabbage stalk]
borago, borage
beta, bete
porrum, leke
alleus, garleke
sinapum, mustarde
lactuta, a letull [lettuce; *MED* does not record sp. *-ull*]
sinapis, mustard sede
siuolus, a chebol [*MED, chibol,* spring-onion]
salgea, tipella, sawge [sage]
petrocillum, percely
rosa, rose
lilium, lely
viola, violett
ditanium, detayne [dittany]
selidonia, selendyne [celandine]
isopus, isoppe [hyssop]
feniculum, fenell
maratrum, fenelsede
serpellum, pellatorye [pellitory, plant resembling yarrow]
vrtica, anetyll [a nettle]
emila, peradilla, dokke
solsequium, marygolde
malua, malowe
lanceola, a ripis [not in *OED*; *lanceola,* spearwort]
buglossa, langdebefe [*langue-de-boeuf*]
ebula, wall worte [wallwort, a term applied to various plants]
ligustrum, primerose
menta, mynte
flos, flowre
folium, lefe

Folio 314b

intulago, wodbynde
cerasum, chery
pomum, appull
prunum, plum
pirum, pere
castania, a chestane [*MED, chesteine,* chestnut tree]
enucleus, carnell [kernel]
nux, a nutt or a nuttre
anelana, walnott
figus, fygge
vua, grape
cornum, hawe
peculum, bolasse [*MED, bolas,* wild plum]
morum, blakkchery
anugdalum, almond
sinoglossa, hertys tonge
eruca, carloke [*MED, cherlok,* wild mustard; however, *eruca,* colewort]
consolida, daysy
edera, yvy
collocasio, horsemynt
sandix, maddyr

tenerum, tansey
maratrum, fenellsede
absinthium, wormewode
plantago, weybrede [*OED, way-bread,* plantain]
narstucium, watyrcars [watercress; *cress* is often metathesized in ME]
crocus, safrowne
piper, pepyr
cinimium, commyn
zinziperium, gyngyr
amonium, canell [*MED, canel,* cinnamon]
liquericia, licoryse [this and the next three herbs occur in the same order in Chaucer's *The Tale of Sir Thopas,* lines 1950-55, which suggests that the poet may have had a glossary such as this one as his source.]
seduarium, sedwary [zedoary]
gariofilus, gelofyr [gillyflower]
cirpus, rysche [rush]
sugura, sugur
macia, mace

Nomina terrarum plantarum
et aliarum rerum
[Names of soils, plants,
and other things]

aier, ayer
terra, the erthe
aqua, limpha, ampnus, mare, pelagus, pontus, a water
stella, sterre
sol, sonne
luna, mone
nubes, nubulum, nebulum, clowde
ventus, wynd
aura, wedyr
bisextus, a lepore [error for *lep-yer* (leap year)?]

Folio 315a

fulgur, lytynnyng
tonitrus, tonitrium, thundyr
dies, daye
nox, nyȝthe
oriens, the est
borias, the northe
austrum, the sowthe
occidens, the weste
quadragesima, lent
natale dium, cristmas
pasca, estur
carniprenium, schrofe tyde
celum, hewyn
paradisus, paradyse
purgatorium, purgatory
infernus, tartarus, hell
mons, hyll
collis, hyll toppe
silua, a wode
pratum, medowe
via, wey
vicus, strete
murus, walle
gleba, clotte [clod]
rupes, sapum, roche
herbarium, viridarium, an erbar[y]
ortus, garden
inclusorium, pynfolde
campus, rus, agrum, felde
firmamentum, firmame[nt]
puppis, nauis, schyppe
malus, maste
rudens, cabull
remus, ower
troclea, wyndasse [*OED, windas,* windlass]
pluuia, rayne
iris, rayne bowe
nix, snowe
grando, hayle
ros, dewe
pruina, hore froste
filandria, gossomer
fons, welle
stagnum, ponde
vmarium, byschoppys ponde
gurges, streme
fossa, fouea, dyche

Folio 315b

furce, galowys [gallows]
forus, forum, mercatum, markett
emptorium, a chepyng [*MED, chepinge,* market]
spelunca, a denne [den, cave]
cemitorium, chyrchȝarde
hernuus, wyldyrnesse
herimitagium, an ermitage
solicitudo, bysynes
villa, pagus, epidum, towne
ciuitas, vrbs, a cyte
abbathia, abbay
hospitale, hospitalle
caracata, plowlonde
virgata, spacium, a ȝarde of londe
pomarium, orcharde
curtilagium, a curtlage [*MED, curtilage,* vegetable garden]
riuus, pisatorium, broke
sepes, hegge
sarifragium, quarell [*OED, quarrel,* sb.[2], quarry]

Nomina vermum
[Names of vermin]

vermis, vermiculus, worme
tinea, mothe
cicada, a grahopper [error for *gras-*]
salamandra, crekett
tarus, brokke [*MED, brok,* n. (1), badger, beaver]
aranea, an addyrcoppe [*MED, attercoppe,* spider]
nocteluca est vermis splendens in nocte [not glossed]
serpens, addyr
coluber, snake
trena, treworme [*OED, tree-worm,* toredo or ship-worm]
brina, hegesson [not in *MED, OED*]
scacraluus, scarbatt [*OED, scarbot,* beetle]
carubius, hollworme [*carubius* apparently = Charybdis (the form *carubdis* occurs) and the Eng. = *hole* (i.e., cave) worm]
erenacius, an vrchun [hedgehog]
culer, gnatt [*culer,* error for *culex*]
musca, flye
pulex, fle
formica, an empte [emmet, ant]
pediculus, lowse
apes, bee
fucus, a drane [drone]
papilio, buttyrflye

Nomina volucrum
[Names of birds]

pauo, pecokke
gallus, cokke

Folio 316a

gallina, henne
gallinucula, henchyke
pullus, chekyn
anca, gose
ancer, gandyr
citacus, popyniay
falco, fawcon
acredula, cardnellus, goldfynche
philomena, nyȝtyngale
castrimargus, wodkokke
fulica, a cutt [*MED, cote,* n. (4), coot]
mauiscus, thrusche
signus, swanne
ardea, heron
faceanus, fesawnte
nisus, sparhauke
irrodius, fawcon
pellicanus, pellicane
aquila, egle
mergus, plouer
nicticorax, nyȝthcrow [*OED, night-crow,* probably an owl or a nightjar]
frigella, redbreste
cornix, crowe
coruus, rauen
regulus, wrenne
alcedo, wodewalle [*OED, woodwall,*

a singing bird, probably the golden oriole]
columba, culuer [dove]
turtur, turtyll [turtledove]
miluus, kyȝte
alauda, larke
hicter, wodwalle [see *alcedo* above]
vltur, gryppe [*MED*, *grip*, n. (3), griffin, vulture; *vltur*, error for *vu*-]
bubo, owyll
vespertilio, reremowse [bat]
perdix, pertryche
irundo, swalowe
palustris, rede sparow
frondator, sterlyng
pica, a pye [*a* followed by *pica*, deleted]
alaudarius, hoby [*MED*, *hobi*, n. (1), small species of hawk]
anas, dukke
anatinus, dukkbyrde [duckling; not in *MED*; *bird* originally referred to the young of any species]
capus, muskett [*MED*, *muskete*, sparrow hawk]
ancipitar, goshauke
tarcellus, tarcelle [*OED*, *tercel*, male of any kind of hawk]

Nomina vestimentorum
[Names of garments]

fururatura, a forer [*MED*, *furrure*, (b), robe or blanket of fur]
ceruical, bolstar
limas, barme cloth [apron]
sindo, sindyll [*OED*, *sendal*, garment of silk]
sericum, sylke
bissis, whyte sylke

Folio 316b

carentinella, a canwas [*MED*, *canevas*, canvas]
stragula, ray [*OED*, *ray*, sb.[4], striped cloth]
panellus, a panell [*MED*, saddle cloth]
sudarium, wyndyng shete
mantica, a male [pouch]
priera, perula, steropp
marcipium, cremena, powche
pulminar, coschun [cushion]
sartabaria, a clenerne [not in *MED*, *OED*; *sart*-, patch, suggests tailor's shop]
paniculum, clowte
armilausa, cloke
scapularium, scapulary
pilius, capp
tena, hofe [*MED*, *houve*, close-fitting cap, coif]
mitra, mityr
mitella, coyffe
crinale, certum, regnum, garlande
corona, crowyn
diadema, dyademe
capellum, hatt
ligula, laynard [*MED*, *lainer*, lace, thong, strap]
corrigia, thonge
caliga, hose
sotularis, scho
pedulus, soccus, sokke
mita, mytane
ciroteca, glove
ocrea, bote
pedana, wampey [*OED*, *vamp*, sock; records sp. *wampe*; *vamp* also = part of a boot or shoe]
intercucium, a walte [*OED*, *welt*, sb.[1], part of shoe]
pictacium, clowte [cloth]
capicium, hode
leripipium, typett [*OED*, *tippet*, strip of cloth hanging from sleeve or hood]
tunica, cote
intima, duplicatura, a linyng
toga, gowne
collobium, tabarde
manica, slefe
fibula, boton

bracce, a bryche [breeches]
alba, albe
stola, stole
amita, examitum, tiaro, amys
fannula, a fanne [*MED, fan,* no meaning in sense of clothing; Lat. *vanna, fanna,* only in the sense of winnowing fan; however, *fanula,* maniple]
superpellicium, surples

Folio 317a

clamis, mantell
mantellus, pallium, mantelle
pannus, vestis, clothe [cloth]
indumentum, a clothyng
supertunica, surcote
epitogium, gowne
roba, robe
cooportorium, a keueryng [*MED, covering,* any piece of clothing; also, an ornament]
tapetum, tapett [*OED, tapet,* piece of figured cloth used as hanging, etc.]
telare, strapyll [*OED, strapple,* covering for lower body with band laced around]
lumbare, lumbatorium, breydegyrdyll [*MED, brey-girdel,* variant of *brech-girdel,* loincloth; see fol. 295b]
vimbria, ora, hemme
fascia, cradylbond
lanicia, rokett [*OED, rochet,* smock, frock, cloak, or mantle]
cinctura, seyme [seam]
gremium, a lappe [*MED, lappe,* 1. (a), lower part of shirt; (b), loose sleeve; 2. folded or extended skirt . . . used as receptacle]
peplum, wympyll
vitta, fylett
culatra, quylte
piracium, a brey [not in *MED*; perhaps *brei* (see *lumbare, . . . breydegyrdyll,* above), breech]

Nomina animalia quadripedum
[Names of four-footed animals]

leo, lyon
leola, lyonesse
ceruus, harte
cerua, hynde
fera, a wyldbeste
crinulus, hinulus, fawne
damus, bukke
dama, doo
lupus, wolfe
lupa, sche wolfe
vrsus, bere
vrsa, sche bere
leopardus, lybarde
vnicornius, vnicorne
vulpes, foxe
taurus, bulle
caper, gote
capra, sche gote
edus, edulus, kyde
hircus, bukke
simea, ape
cuniculus, conye
furo, ferrett
elephas, olyfawnte [*elephas,* altered from *l*-]
scurrellus, squyrell

Folio 317b

sirogrillus, squyrell
mustela, wesyll
bos, ox
vacca, vaccula, cowe
bouiculus, bullokke
asinus, asella, asse
azellus, lytyll asse
iuuenca, heyfer
vitulus, calfe [altered from *cafe*]
camellus, camell
equus, horse
equa, mare
iuuentum, a helpyng beste
caballas, cabyll [*MED, cabel,* horse]
dextarius, stede

succussarius, trottar
gradale, amblar
pullus, colte
sus, porca, scropha, sowe
porcus, swyne
porcellus, pygge
agnus, lambe
aper, bore
ouis, schepe
aries, wedyr
viredus, carte horse
canis, dogge
caniculus, kenett [*MED, kenet,* small hunting dog]
leporarius, grehownde
odornisecus, spaynell
gregarius, cur dogge
catulus, whelpe
molosus, taydogge [not in *OED*; *molosus, molussus,* hound, bandog (watchdog)]
lecista, byche
catus, mureligus, catte
lepus, hare
rato, ratte
mus, mowse [*mus* added above]
talpa, molle
bufo, tode
rans, frogge

Nomina diuersarum domorum
[Names of various buildings]

monasterium, monastery
ecclesia, chyrche
templum, tempyll
castrum, castell

Folio 318a

opidum idem [glosses preceding entry]
turris, towre
capella, chapell
casa, casula, lytyll howse
domus, edes, howse
aula, hall
cancelle, chansell
camera, talamus, conchinius, chambyr
celarium, selar
solarium, soler
panta, prouituarium, pincernaculum, pantry
lardarium, lardyr
despensatorium, penu, spense
taberna, caupona, taverne
granatorium, garner
orrium, barne
porcorium, ara, swynstye
tegerium, magale, sheperdis howse
coquina, kechyn
stabulum, stabyll
carcer, prisone
hospicium, an yn
fornax, furnace
lupanar, bordelhowse [The sequence of entries beginning here is significant, since *fornax* (*fornix*), the preceding entry, was a euphemism for a bordello]
ouile, caula, fowlde [sheepfold]
fabrica, aurifociu[m], forge
gallinarium, hennekope
locutorium, parlowre
precepe, crache [*MED, cracche,* manger]
mollendinum, myll
claustrum, clowster
dormitorium, dortor
tabernaculum, tabernacle
lanificium, a wall howse [wool house]
cloaca, a wardrope [privy (a euphemism)]
latrina, cathacumba, galfabie, a prive [privy]
bostar, oxestalle
intentorium, a tentor [*OED, tenter,* frame on which cloth is dried; here, the structure housing such a frame]
pinstrinum, bake house
pandoxatorium, bruehose [brew

house]

Folio 318b

palacium, pales [palace]

Nomina diuersarum rerum
existencium in falcatoria
et aurifoncia
[Names of various things
found in the scythemaker's
and goldsmith's shops]

incus, an anwylde [anvil]
malleus, hamer
forceps, payr of tongis
aspersorium, a sprynkyll [*OED*, *sprinkle*, 1. a., sprinkler]
follis, a below [bellows]
scoria, syndyr [cinder; slag]
clauis, clauiculus, nayle
sarra, saw
ferrus, horsschoo
lima, a wayle [file; see *folen*, fol. 339b]
crusta, crustula, a bose [*MED*, *boce*, boss]
lamina, lama, a plate [layer of metal]
planetorium, a planer [*OED*, *planer*, 3., instrument for smoothing]
tolus, pomell
capulus, hylte
manubrium, hafte
sindula, blade
epirasinus, a tonge
cultellus, knyfe

Nomina rerum ecclesiarum
[Names of ecclesiastical things]

altare, an autyr
superaltare, a superaltare
vestiarium, vestibulum, vestry
crux, crucula, a crosse
crucifixus, crucifixe
fons, a faut [font; error for *faunt*?]
imago, image
gradus, a grese [*MED*, *gre*, n. (1), one of the gradual Psalms; *grese* (not in *MED*) a collection of these Psalms]
portiforium, a portuyse [*OED*, *portas*, portable breviary]
missale, missall
gradale, grayle [gradual]
troparium, tropar
calendarium, calendar
imnarium, an ymnar [hymnal]
letania, letany
antiphinarium, an antifonar
primarium, a primar
psalterium, sawter [psalter]
martilogium, martloge [*MED*, *martiloge*, martyrology]
biblia, bibliotecha, a bybyll
manuale, manuell
passionarium, a passionar [*OED*, *passional*, book relating the sufferings of saints and martyrs]

Folio 319a

registrum, a register
ordinale, an ordinall
calix, chales [chalice]
patena, paten
corporale, corporas [*MED*, *corperas*, altar cloth]
fiola, cruett [*MED*, *cruet*, small vessel for sacramental wine]
pixis, boxe
ostia, eucaristia, an obley [*MED*, *oble*, bread or wafer used in the sacrament]
sacrarium, a sacryng [*OED*, *sacring*, 1. b., the consecrated objects]
campana, campanella, belle
batilla, clapyr
thurribulum, acerra, sensar
thus, thimiama, incensum, sense [incense]
feretrum, libitina, loculus, a bere [bier; see fol. 14b]
campanile, campanarium, bellhowse

candelabrium, candylstykke
cera, wex
candela, candyll
lichinus, weke [wick]
cereus, tapyr
vitrum, glasse
tronus, a trone
tumba, cercophagus, mansolium, sepulcrum, grave [*mansolium*, error for *mau-*]
petra, lapis, stone
crismatorium, crismatory
armariolum, an almary [*MED, almerie*, place for storing, or safekeeping]
funus, corda, cordicula, corde
fidis, harpestrenge
oleum, oyle
lampas, lampe
organum, an organe
pinaculum, pynacle [*OED* gives no special ecclesiastical sense]
cambucca, a cambuke [*MED, camboke*, curved stick (?), glossed *pedum*; some confusion with next entry?]
pedum, a clupe [*MED, clip*, n. (1), iron rod with hook for lifting or suspending pots; however, *pedum* could mean crosier]
lacerna, a lanterne [*lacerna*, error for *lanterna*]
spectaculum, a spectacule [*OED, spectacle*, 5., window or mirror]
lectrinum, a dexe [*MED, desk*, lectern; records sp. *dex*]

Nomina metallorum

Folio 319b

aurum, golde
aureus, al of golde
auratus, ouyr gylte
argentum, syluer
argenteus, syluyry
argentatus, syluyrd
es, brasse
ereus, eueus, brasyn
stannum, tynne
cuprum, copyr
cupreus, al of copyr
plumbum, lede
plumbeus, ledde
plumbatus, ledyd
calibs, stele
calibeus, stele
calibatus, stelyd
electrum, pewter
auricalcum, laten [mixed metal, such as brass]
ferrum, irun
ferreus, irun
ferratus, yrundyd
quadrans, fardyng
obolus, halpeny
oblatus, halpenyworthe
gemma, precious stone
gegas, a chete [error for *cheste*?]
cristallum, cristallum [error for *-all*]
margarita, a precious stone
spinter, brest broche
firmaculum, monile, broche
annulus, ryng
nola, belle
bacca, perle
galea, helme
lorica, haburionne [haburgeon, coat of mail]
scutum, schylde
perma, bokeler
pelta, talbas [not in *OED*; *pelta*, small, moon-shaped shield; perhaps named for one of the John Talbots, English soldiers who died late in the fifteenth century]
lancea, spere
telum, darte
arcus, bow
sagitta, arow
iaculum, darte
petilium, bolte
catapulta, brodearowe

torquea, a patre [not in *OED*; perhaps a machine of battle, or the twisted cord used on a catapult]
nodus, knott

Folio 320a

This folio should evidently follow fol. 312b, which begins a list of women's names.
commitessa, cowntes
domina, lady
domicella, damsel
virgo, puella, mayde
femina, mulier, woman
vxor, coniunx, sponsa, wyfe
fabrissa, a smythys wyfe
abatissa, abbas
priorissa, prioresse
mater, genitrix, modyr
filia, dowter
soror, syster
ancilla, handmayde
meretrix, strumpett
compater, godfadyr
commater, materna, godmodyr
paterfamilias, the gode man of the howse
materfamilias, the gode wyfe of the howse
monialis, a nonne
vidua, wydow
rustica, feldmannys wyfe
filatrix, spynster [one who spins]
anugerula, pulteryswyfe
lotrix, candidaria, lawnder
mataxatrix, hecheler [not in *MED*; however, *hechelen,* to comb flax]
vstrinatrix, dryster [*MED, driere, driestere,* one who dries and bleaches cloth]
seriatrix, sewter [*OED, sewster,* seamstress; no sp. without *-s-*]
androchia, dey [*MED, daie,* woman in charge of milking]
pectrix, kembesterre [*MED, kembestere,* comber of wool or flax]
vetula, anus, an oldewyfe
pistrix, bakksterre
pandoxatrix, bruster
pronuba, bawde
obstetrix, mydwyffe

Nomina arborum frugum et earundem fructuum
[Names of fruit-bearing trees and of the fruits themselves]

arbor, tre
pomus, appultre
pirus, pere tre
acer, a mapulltre [*a,* altered from *an*]
prunus, plummetre
quercus, oke
corulus, hasyll
tremulus, an aspe [*MED, aspe* (the common sp.) aspen]

Folio 320b

pinus, pynapultre
laurus, loreltre
palma, palmetre
vlinus, elmetre
salix, welowtre
fagus, byche tre
letiscus, byrche
cornus, hawtre
spinus, thornetre
popular, popelertre
abies, firtrc
taxus, ewtre [yew tree]
fraxinus, aschetre
sambucus, holyntre [perhaps error for *holytre* (holly tree) or *(h)olyutre* (olive tree); *sambucus,* elder]
ebur, an elow tre [not in *MED*; willow? *ebur,* ivory; *OED,* yellow-wood (tree), first cit., seventeenth century]
labrista, wodebynd
arbutus, crabtre
tilia, lyne tre [linden]
viburnus, a nawtre [not in *MED,*

s.v. *a-*, *n-*; *viburnus*, wayfaring tree]
cerasus, cheritre
concanus, concanester [not in *MED*]
castania, chastanetre [chestnut]
ficus, fygtre
anelana, walnott tre
vitus, wyne tre [*OED*, *vine-tree*, vine; blackthorn, mountain ash]
boxus, boxtre
frumentum, whete
seligigo, rye
auena, ote
pisa, pese
faba, a bene
vicia, feche [vetch]
ordium, barly
granificium, brasium, barlymalte [*barly* partly deleted]
lupinus, drawker [*MED*, *drauk*, weed]
dragetum, drage [*MED*, *drage*, see *drauk* (weed)]
zizania, darnell
palea, acus, chaffe
segisterium, draffe [refuse from grains]
messes, seges, bladum, granum, fruges, corne
[fri]bulus, bryer
cardo, thystyll
radix, rote
festuca, atthonius, mote [*OED*, *mote*, 4., single straw, stalk]
nodus, knott
arista, a pelyng of corne
spica, an ere
merica, a brome

Folio 321a

This folio evidently bound out of order; see fol. 313b, which begins the catalogue of fish.]
silurus, fimenlus, roche
vronoscopus, a ray
congrus, congyr
glaucus, whytyng
bolbus, a colle [not in *MED*]
fingia, stokkfyche
turtur, turbutt
tanidrus, styklyng [stickleback]
ragadia, ray
hamus, vncius, a hoke [hook]
rethe, reticulum, nett
squama, scale [fish scale]

Nomina rerum pertinencia rustico
[Names of farm implements]

biga, quadriga, carte
currus, a chare [*MED*, *char*, n. (2), 2, cart]
plaustrum, weyne [wain, wagon]
axis, axtre [axletree]
meditillum, timpanum, an asse stoke [axle stock]
cantus, radius, spoke
limo, cartstaffe
aratrum, plow
herpica, harow
traha, pecten, slyde [*OED*, *slide*, 4. a., kind of sledge (first cit., late seventeenth century); *traha*, sledge; *pecten*, weaver's sley]
themo, plowbeme
collarium, colar
capistrum, halter
capisterius, halterer
buris, plowbeme
s[t]ina, a stilke [*OED*, *stilking*, some part of the gear of a plow (earliest and only cit., sixteenth century)]
iugum, yoke
gerusa, a gode [goad]
ferratorium, plumel [not in *OED*; perhaps *plinnel*]
phalere, horse harn[es]
subtela, autela, peytrell, croper [*croper* added in error? (see next entry); *peytrell*, *OED*, *peitrel*, armor for horse's breast]
postela, cropar [crupper]
dolabrum, brode axe
bipennis, twybyll [two-edged ax]

securis, hachett
terebrum, terebellum, persor [piercer]
celtis, chesell

Folio 321b

trabes, beme
dentale, a groun of a plowe [*MED*, *groin*, n. (1), snout, nose (incl. sp. *groune*); no figurative senses; the meaning is evidently "plowshare"]
scopar, besome [broom]
flagellum, flayll
manutentum, hand staffe
fermipedia, a leste [shoemaker's or saddlemaker's last]
atramentum, bleche [*MED*, *blacche*, black pigment or dye]
formula, forma, a forme [shoemaker's or saddlemaker's form]
sella, sadyll
muscipula, trappe [(mouse)trap]
stramen, strawe
storium, sternolum, matt
sen[]nectorium, barow
pix, pyche [pitch, tar]
pegma, a babyll [*MED*, *babel*, n. (1) (a), toy; (b) jester's scepter (glossed *pigma*)]
scitorium, pedica, panter [*OED*, *panter*, fowler's net]
acies, a scherpnesse of an axe [*a* altered from *an*]
sera, serula, lokke
vectus, repagulum, barre
vanga, spade
tribula, schowyll
ligo, marra, mattoke
frenum, brydell
camus, lupatum, barnacle [*MED*, *bernacle*, n. (1), snaffle-bit]
scaber, buttur [not in *MED*; *OED*, *butteris*, farrier's tool for paring hooves]
stancile, steroppe
cultellus, knyffe
artanus, penknyff
vomer, schare [plowshare]
sarculum, wedehoke [weed hook]
culter, culter
falx, facicula, hoke
calcar, sporre
stimulus, pryke
strepa, styroppe
strigilus, horse kombe
mensacula, brede knyffe
singula, thonge
vncula, bokyll
pluscula, bokyll
acuperium, cos, whettstone
gladius, ensis, swerde
aurifugium, goldwyer [*aurifrigium*, orphrey, gold embroidery]
simina, gold stone

Folio 322a

Nomina rerum pertinencium vxor
[Names of things
pertaining to the housewife]

colus, dystaffe
fusus, spyndyll
mataxa, hechell [*MED*, *hechel*, instrument for carding flax]
uirgillium, demollitorium, yere wyndese [*yere*, apparently an error for *yern*; *OED*, *windas*, windlass; when used for yarn, *windle*; no entry for *yarn windlass*]
canobuam, hempe
linum, flex
filum, threde
glomus, glomicellus, globus, clewe [ball of yarn]
lapsum, a topp [*OED*, *top*, 2., portion of flax put on a distaff]
pensum, ȝarne
foluculus, linodium, lyne betyll [*MED*, *lin*, flax; *betel*, bat; no entry for *lin betel*]
linarium, lynsede

rupa, rupula, roche [*OED*, *rock*, sb.[2], distaff; but *rupa*, *-ula*, rock (stone)]
excudium, swyngyll stokke [*OED*, *swingle*, bat for beating flax; no *swyngyll stokke* recorded]
stupa, herdys [*MED*, *herde*, n. (3), "hard," coarse part of flax]
naperta [not glossed]
limpulus, a strykaflyne [*OED*, *strick*, bundle of hemp; apparently = *strick-of-linen*]
stodarium, stodell [*OED*, *studdle*, 2., upright post of a loom]
alabrum, rele
troilia, trendyll [error for *tredyll*]
lamia, pecten, a sley [*OED*, *slay*, sb.[1], weaving instrument to beat up the weft; see *glythe*, fol. 176a]
licinatorium, slykstone [*OED*, *sleekstone*, used for smoothing and polishing cloth]
liciatorium, webbeyme [*OED*, *web-beam*, roller on a loom]
turma, subtegmen, wefte
stamen, warpe
forago, lyste [*MED*, *liste*, n. (2), border]
lac, mylke
buturum, botur
caseus, chese
quaccus, creme
corum, whey
balductum, possett [*OED*, *posset*, drink of hot milk, wine, spices]
coagulum, curde
collustrum, a bustyng [*beesting(s)*, first milk secreted by a cow after calving; *a*, followed by *f* (deleted)]
ficella, chesefatt [cheese vat]
ventilabrum, wedyrkoc

Nomina rerum pertinencia aule
[Names of things
pertaining to a house]

mensa, tabyll
scannum, benge [bench; *MED* does not record *-g-* spelling]
cathedra, cheyr
tristella, tripos, trestyll
scaccarium, a cheker [chessboard]
hostium, dore
autica, wykett [gate]
gumphus, a priuy [this entry begins a series dealing with things associated with rooms; therefore, the privy is thought of as indoors (behind a partition); *gumphus* seems to be a comical term but occurs elsewhere]
ligatura, bonde

Folio 322b

repagulum, dore barre
fenestra, fenestrella, wyndow
paries, muris, walle
scale, laddyr
foramen, hole
later, tyle stone
marmur, marbull
veru, verutum, a spytt [spit (for cooking); *verutum*, spear, lance]
gipsum, mortar
acer, a lathe [*lath*; *acer* = *asser*]
viscus, lyme
absconsa, sconse
discus, dysche
talus, taxillus, lea, a dyse [dice (die)]
postica, posterula, posterne
venticubilum, porche
ianua, porta, a ȝate
angulus, corner
ignius, fyyr
domicilium, howsholde
limen, thresscholde
aulium, docer [*MED*, *doser*, tapestry]
focale, fewell [*MED*, *feuel*, fuel]
curtina, curteyne
lodium, lauacrum, a lavyr [*MED*, *lavour*, (a) pitcher; (b) washbasin; lavatory in a cloister]
pelius, basyne
lauacrum, lauatorium, a lavyr

portica, porche
fax, foculus, bronde [brand, torch]
forma, a schappe [*OED*, *shape*, 14. a., mold for cookery; first cit., eighteenth century]
repofocilum, a wonderyn [not in *OED*; the ending *-eryn* perhaps = *iron*, thus a variant of *andiron*; see fol. 148a, *andyrun*; *Promptorium parvulorum* (col. 351) glosses *repofocilium* as "plate of a fyyr erth" (col. 351), a fire-clay tile]
scutella, plater
periapsis, dubler [*MED*, *doubler*, plate or platter]
potagiarium, potyngere [*OED*, *pottinger*, porringer]
salsarium, sawser [*OED*, *saucer*, dish for salt or sauces]
cacabus, lebes, caudrun [caldron]
patella, panne
sartago, fryyng panne
mola, querne [mill, handmill]
creagra, fleschoke [fleshhook]
pilus, pestelle
tripos, trevett
carbo, prima, cole
cathena, cheyne
viviolus, posnett [*OED*, *posnet*, small metal pot for boiling]

Folio 323a

puls, potage
brodium, brothe
papatum, brothe
polenta, flowre
adipatum, brues [*MED*, *broues*, broth]
latea, blawmange [blancmange]
tucetum, a podyng [sausage]
omentu, omasus, trype
ferina, a wensonne [venison, flesh of any game animal]
nucatorium, a grater
dormicio, dormitacio, sopor, somnus, slepe
lectus, lectulus, thorus, grabatum, bedde
animal, bestia, pecus, pecus, a beste [*pecus* repeated]
ouis, veruex, badeus, aries, weddyr
muto, multo, bilanx, schepe
semita, limes, trames, orbita, casus, via, pathe
catus, catulus, pilax, mureligus, catt
bladum, seges, fruges, messis, far, annona, corne
cibus, esca, commestus, commestio, prandum, epulum, dapes, mete

Folio 323b

cibarium, mete
potus, potacio, ceruisia, selia, ale [*ceruisia*, altered from *s*-]
vinum, temetum, libum, bachus, falernum, merum, mustum, wyne
tristicia, mesticia, dolor, molestia, vlulatus, planctus, meror, gemitus, suspirium, sorowe
suspirium, pyntil [penis; added in a different hand; it is not clear that *suspirium* is the word being glossed]
societas, coniuna, legio, sodalium, turba, turmus, collegium, phalanx, consorcium, contuberinum, a company
societas, arse lyk[e] [added in a different hand; it is not clear that *societas* is the word being glossed; the intended sense is arse-lick; the proximity of breeches, love, and the devil is suggestive]
bracce, femorale, perizonia, a breche [breeches]
amor, dilectio, zelus, caritas, feruor, love
mora, aiunta, permansio, ounta,

a taryyng
festinacio, properacio, materacio, acceleracio, velocitas, celeritas, a hying [hieing, hastening]
diabolus, demon, cacademon, apostata, belial, the dewyll [devil]

Folio 324a

satan, pluto, dis, sumanus, the dewyll [devil]
lucifer, altudo, sublimitas, precordium, fastidium, hynesse [*lucifer,* belongs in preceding series]
liber, libellus, codex, volumen, pagina, boke
munnisina, moneta, pecunia, census, es, mony
canistrum, cophinus, sporta, sportula, corbus, calathus, baschett
desertum, heremus, solitudo [not glossed]

Nomina villarum
[Names of cities]

[Added in a different hand]
romagus, rotomagus, rome
gallia, francia, frawnce
dorabarnia, cantueria, cantyrbery
pannonia, lumbardy
anglia, britania, ynglond
couentria, coventre
bristollia, brystow [Bristol]
cantabrigia, cambryg
oxonis, oxynford
deuonia, devynshyre [altered (illegible)]
villa, opidum, pagus, towne
vintonia, vynchester
vigorina, vorcerter [error for *vorcester* (Worcester)? but cf. *glouerina* . . . *glocetter,* following entry]
glouerina, glocestria, glocetter
septrina, shaftebery
dinolinia, dyrham [added in a later hand: *lindfinera idem est*]
normania, neustra, normandy
parisius, parys
exonia, excetyr

Folio 324b

ardea, a herne [heron; the shift to birds suggests that a folio is out of order; a list of birds begins on fol. 315b]
ibis, snyte [*OED, snite,* snipe]
statura, stature
superficies, þe over part
nuber, schowre
diuicue, ryches
seges, granum, semen, corne
apollo, titan, phebus, eoos, sone [*eoos, Eos,* dawn; glossed as if it were an Eng. word]
orrea, barne
edulium, sule [*OED, saulee,* satisfying meal, quantity of food]
edulius, kokney [*MED, cokenei,* n. (2), pampered child; *OED, cockney,* 2, child that sucketh long; the sense of overeating or being pampered with food is implied here]
innamen, lykyng [*MED, liking,* 1. b., sexual pleasure, the sense perhaps intended here; the Lat. provides no clue]
dilectio, delyth [delight]
celer, hevenly
opus, nede
ebdomada, septimana, woke [week]
vicium, vyce
parasitus, gluto, comedo, nebulo, lego, nando, glotyn
insanea, woddnes [madness, insanity]
cominium, lordshyp
exemium, presant [present, gift]
macherus, koke [cook]
machera, a dressyng knyfe
catarrus, þe poose [*OED, pose,* sb.[1],

cold in the head]
instator, mercator, marchaunte
quactum, creme
mel, hunny
qualus, payner [pannier, basket]
aratrum, plowe
iconomus, husbond man [husbandman, farmer]
marcipium, powche
norma, rewle
cirurgicus, surgyn
selus, a syn
iter, iurney
remuneracio, rewarde
edes, howse
sumptus, cost
zelus, enuiy [*MED*, *envy*, jealousy]
mensura, mesure
culina, papina, kychyn
addiscere, a lernyng
facestia, vrbanitas, curtesy
iocale, iuell [jewel; *iocale*, perhaps error for *ioculare*]
porrigo, þe poxe [pox, a term used for a variety of diseases; *porrigo*, scruff, dandruff]
ferina, vensunn [venison, flesh of any game animal]
acetum, acromacium, vargis [*OED*, *verjuice*, juice of green or unripe fruit]

Folio 325a

discolus, truant
nucatatorium, a grate [grater]
tegula, tylle [tile]
cementum, mortar
iemeus, bruma, wyntyr
gelu, froste
operarius, worke man
pedica, lutum, panter [*OED*, *panter*,[1] fowler's net]
lutum, coccinum, scarlett [cloth (not always red)]
pictaciator, cobler
comedum, persett [not in *OED*; *comedum*, feast]
egritudo, infirmitas, sekenesse
squinancia, quynce [quinsy]
audacia, boldnesse
statem, grossum, grote [*MED*, *grot*, n. (3), groat, 4 pence]
mercinomium, morsis, marchandry [*MED*, *marchaundrie*, trading]
toga, ropa, gowne
pilliparius, skynner
ius, ryȝt
desidia, accidia, signicia, marca, torbor, slothe
malagma, emplastrum, plastyr [plaster (applied to the skin as a curative)]
cerotum, salue
merda, stercus, a torde
concitudo, ritus, custum
ipopante, purificacio, purificacioun
adragia, day [*MED*, *daie*, woman in charge of milking]
multrale, payle
crepuscula, euyntyde
mango, scorser [*OED*, *scorser*, one who exchanges or barters; first cit., 1531]

Nomina pissium
[Names of fish]

vranoscopus, þornebake [*OED*, *thornback*, ray or skate]
ragadia, raye
molanurus, merlyng [merling, whiting]
palanudes, playce [plaice]
capito, gurnarde [*MED*, *gurnard*, any of European gurnards]
foca, porpeys
mirena, lamprey [(sea) *lamprey*]
lamperda, lamprynne [*MED*, *lamproun*, river lamprey (cf. preceding entry)]
morus, myllewell [*MED*, *mulwel*, codfish]
mullolus [not glossed]

megarius, makerell
blanccus, why [evidently the beginning of *whytefysche*]
rumbus, sturgeoun
salmo, samon

Folio 325b

ostrium, oyster
congrinis, congour
finigia, stokfysse
allec, heryng, salt fysshe
conchile, kokell
musculus, muscull, welke
solia, solefyssche
squama, scale [(fish) scale]
polupus, lopster
ephimera, sperlyng [*OED*, *sparling*, smelt]
angville, elle [eel]
cancer, crabe
lucus, luce
canica, hownfysshe [dogfish]
cetus, whale
dentrix, pyke
dentricula, pykerell [altered from *pykelell*]
pecten, playce [plaice]
truda, trowte
cilurus, loche [loach]
turbo, turbote
gobio, gogyun [*MED*, *gojoun*, gudgeon]
sprottus, sprott [sprat]
falco, facoun [falcon]
alendarius, hoby [*MED*,*hobi*, n. (1), small species of hawk]
nisus, sparhawke
alietus, gentyllhawke [noble hawk; *MED*, *gentil*, adj., 3. (b), applied to birds]
hirecius, goshawke
tarcelus, tarcell [*OED*, *tercel*, male of any kind of hawk]
capus, musket [*MED*, *muskete*, sparrow hawk]
incolatus, dwellyng place
scotegina, scott [entry begins a short list of foreigners associated with lowlife (*keler of lyse* below) and criminals (*pursketer* below)]
flawdrigina, flemmyng
icornibigina, cornysman
coesigina, a man of greke
ibernigina, hyrysman [Irishman]
mesipita, harvystman
lencida, keler of lyse [killer of lice]
bursicida, pursketer [pursecutter, thief]
plenilunium, þe full mone
nouilunium, neomenia, newe mone
vastum, commyn felde
moracia, a cob nott [*MED*, *cobel-nut*, variety of hazelnut; no sp. *cob* recorded]
paragraphus, a false wrytt[er]
paragraphia, a falce wrytyng
pietancia, a petawnce [*OED*, *pittance*, pious donation to a religious house or order]
farum, a crane of a wharfe [perhaps tower on a wharf; *pharus*, tower, lighthouse; *crane* as a mechanical contrivance not recorded until eighteenth century]

Folio 326a

bipennis, polox [poleax]
pigro, baslard [*MED*, *baselard*, dagger]
piteso, bacoun [error for *batoun*, stick, club]
lapista, goddard [*MED*, *godard*, earthenware pot or bowl]
cupa, cowle [*MED*, *covel*, tub, vat]
alitrigium, a cade of heryng [*MED*, *cade*, n. (1), barrel (for herring)]
acedo, a culmowse [*MED*, *cul-mose*, kingfisher]
creaga, fleshoke [fleshhook]
eriductile, structura, wyre
stirillum, gotis berd [goatsbeard,

plant]
lambutum, lute [*MED, lute,* n. (2), clay]
ponduca, b[?]pype
carista, a derth of corne or whete
venecisium, wycshecrafte [witchcraft; *venecisium* (veneficium), sorcery, preparation of magic potions]
seruitus, seruys
dessencio, departe [*MED, depart,* departure, separation; no sense of dispute]
homicidium, mans slawtyr
mansuetudo, mekenes
quietudo, esse [ease]
inquietudo, dysses [disease, discomfort]
obsides, presoner
septemuum, vij ȝer age [seven years of age]
septemus, vij ȝe olde [a seven-year-old; *ȝe,* error for *ȝer*]
lienteria, þe flyx [flux; *lien,* spleen]
barrica, hogais hede [error for *hoggis hede*]
comfortacio, consolanie, consolacio, solamen, insolamen, comforte
racio, raciocinium, rekenyng
debere, devyr [*MED, dever,* duty]
iuridicus, legisperitus, legisperitor, iurista, a man of law
canonista, of cannon law
superfacta, forissuperfacta, surfet
smigma, sope [soap; altered from *sape*]
pix, pyche
picius, dark as pyche
septentreonarius, aquilo, boreas, sepentreo, þe northe [*septentreonarius,* altered from *sem-*]
theologia, vtilitas, devynete [divinity]
consuetudo, comodum, proficuum, emolimentum, profectus, a prophete [profit; *consuetudo* deleted]

Folio 326b

parasive, goodfryday
spacium, intervallum, tempus, mora, divturnitas, spase
bunecius [not glossed]
solinolus, selevyllye [not in *OED*; preceded by *ewylly* (deleted)]
laicus, prophanus, agramatus, illiteratus, leyman
exoticus, vn kynd [unnatural]
negligens, incuriosus, incunirus, rechylys or negligens [error for *negligent*; *rechylys,* reckless]
turrenda, turestina, brownebrede
solers, assiduus, bysy
fretus, vndyr sett [supportive; *fretus,* relying upon]
antipera, a scryne [screen]
tripos, trestellus, a trestell [*a* altered (illegibly)]
sponda, formula, a furme [*MED, form,* 3. c., bench]
igniarium, focarium, herthe

Folio 327a

calefactorium, a chafer [*MED, chafour,* vessel for heating water]
exedra, bay wyndow
lucar, lodium, a lowuer [*MED, lover,* n. (1), small structure on roof for venting smoke or admitting light]
ligatura, bonde
fenestrale, fenestrall [*MED, fenestral,* window]
acer, lath
absconsa, a sconse
aulium, a doscer [*MED, doser,* tapestry]
foculus, idem est que fax [not glossed]
potagiarium, a poyntynger [error for *poyt-*? porringer]
lapista, a cruys [*MED, crouse,*

earthen pot]
Equs meus est redorsatus, gallyd, **et acclauatus est,** a cloyyd [*MED*, *a cloien*, maim or cripple]
placenta, a wygge [*placentula*, bun; perhaps wedge-shaped cake]
clitella, burþan [burden]
librella, gunne [*MED*, *gonne*, 1., siege engine that casts missiles; (2), cannon; the latter sense is probably intended here]
sincopis, a sownyng [swooning]
narstucium, cars [cress (plant)]
voniellus, a chap of a scheyth [*MED*, *chape*, metal mounting for a scabbard]
vaccinium, cowslope [cowslip; *-lope* is a common spelling]
ligustrum, plym rose [primrose; *OED* does not record sp. *pl-*, which may be an error]
incenis, soperlys [supperless]
surculus, a graffe [shoot, twig]
iste homo est dapsilis discibo et potu, large [gloss misplaced, belonging to next entry]
protegus, large
potende [not glossed]

Folios 327b–328a

Latin numerals; no English glosses.

Folio 328b

defecatus, stale ale[*defecatus*, defecated, purified; perhaps intended as a humorous gloss]
solers, wyty [intelligent]

Folio 329a

semis, halfe
semimortu[us], halfedede
semiuiuus, halfe qwyke [half-alive]
ferox, crudelis, trux, atrox, seuus, seuerus, cruell
manticapalis, malapert
crassus, incrassatus, sagmatus, inpinguatus, fatte
macer, macilentus, lene
colibertus, natiuus, bonde [not free]
liberatus, liber, fre
vterque, eydyr eydyr [either, or]
pronitus, redy
loquendus, to be spoke
verax, trew
mitis, pius, meke
liberus, fre entryng [*entryng* misplaced, belonging with next entry, where it is repeated]
introitus, entring
versus, curuyng [curving]
intensus, grett hette [great heat]
cerebrosus, vnwytty [ignorant; *cerebrosus*, insane]
infinitus, endles
legitimus, licitus, lawfull
iniquus, wykkyd
dilegens, dylygent [altered from *-eng*]
astutus, wyly
mundanis, mundanus, wordly [worldly; *OED* does not list *wordly* as a legitimate sp. variant]
immensus, grett
fededignus, trew man
continuus, by and by [*MED*, *bi and bi*, (b), continually]
ieiunus, fastyng
ieiunabilis, fastyng day
lesus, hurte [*lesus*, wailing, funeral lamentation]
scientificus, sciens, cunnyng [intelligent]
infirmus, eger, seke [sick]
ebes, optusus, dull
penulatus, forde [furred]
attonatus, stounde [*OED*, *stound*, v.[2], stupefy; this would appear to be past part.]
fedus, full [vile (*foedus*, vile); *OED* records sp. *file*]

labes, macula, spotte

Folio 329b

susceptus, lene
siticulosus, sitibundus, thursty
sepedus, curtese [courteous]
famelicus, huggury [error for *hunggury*?]
ambroninus, lycores [lecherous]
sepe, sepius, frequenter, multociens, plerumque, pluries vt plurielicenter, oftyntymys

Ad verbia
[Adverbs]

subdiuo, þerowȝt [*OED*, *therout*, 2., out of doors]
prius, be fore
perantia, propriuus, herbefore
libenter, gladly
pallominus, all most [*pallominus*, *paulo minus*, lit. "less by a little"]
fere, pene, ferme, idem sunt [gloss preceding entry, in a later hand]
precipue, saltim, namly [*MED*, *nam(e)li*, 1. (a), especially; 2. (a), specifically]
nedum, not only
nullicubi, no where
fideliter, verasiter, vere, trewly
absque, sine, with owȝt
fene, fere, all most
paulominus, ferme, id est fere [not glossed]
nanci, naut [nought]
omnino, penitus, att alle
indesinenter, vn sesynly [unceasingly]
subito, repentine, cito, cicissime, suple, sudenly
amodo, fro hens forward
hucusque, actiuus, hedyr to
vix, vn neth [scarcely]
quin, but þat
crudeliter, cruely
licenter, lawfully
parce, scasly [scarcely; *scasly* error for *scarsly*?]
demum, tandem, att þe last
vulgo, plane, distincte opunly
vtrumque, ne, an, putas, wyther [whether]
eciam [not glossed]
rim[?]o, perfiemo, enim, etenim, for soþe
muniatim, all of pecis
inposterum, her after
aliter, oþor wyse
tum, what
alibi, or els wher
tamen, attamen, verumptamen, nichillomnus, nevyr þe lesse
modo, iam, nudum, quondam, inpresenciarum, nunc, now
hauspicato, nedys coste [necessarily]

Folio 330a

[Deleted]
Nomina adiectiua
[Names of adjectives; deleted]
Verba sunt
[Verbs; added in a later hand]

meto, to rype
maturesco, waxe rype
confudo, to shame
afficio, couet
licio, to be set by [evaluated]
liceor, to preysye [appraise]
bacor, to waxe woode [go mad]
conuersor, comitabor, to drawe to [join (a group)]
renuncio, abronuncio, to for sake
illudo, to scorne
affligo, torqueor, to torment
castigo, corripio, to shaste [chasten]
indago, to serche

placo, make esy [*MED, esi,* 3., peaceable, calm]
sanxio, dico, sacrifico, santifico, to hawlow [hallow]
valeo, to fare
preualeo, to be more worth
miror, stupeor, to meruell
erogo, distrubuo, to dele [apportion]
lucubro, to wake be candelyȝt
intoxico, to puosyn [poison]
moror, commoror, maneo, permane, to dwell [linger, delay]
vlciccor, to venge, venyawnce [*vlciccor,* followed by *owȝt lawe* (deleted)]
placito, religo, proscribo, to owȝt lawe
populor, consummo, devasto, to waste [lay waste]
permitto, suffero, pacior, sino, fero, tolero, suffyr [allow]
compello, ango, vrgeo, angorior, cogo, arcio, arto, constringo, to constrayn
exploro, to a spy [espy]

Folio 330b

vil[i]pendo, pompendo, naucipendo, nichillpendo, floxpendo, to sett lytyll by
expergiscor, to wake owȝt of slepe
recolo, reminiscor, recordo, to remembyr [*recordo,* altered from *-or*]
frunio, to tanne
horreo, formido, metuo, paueo, [ti]meo, vereor, to dred
negosior, marcandiso, marcor, to do marchandyse
animo, to make bold
comparo, emo, to by
venundo, vendo, sell
veneo, be sold
susurro, to rownd in þe ere [*rownd,* whisper]
excorcico, to pyll garlyc [*pyll,* peel]
conspicor, to loke downe
obsideo, to ley a sechyd [lay a siege, besiege]
gipso, to plastyr
obiurgor, lixor, to chyd
clamito, clalannge [error for *challange*? *OED. clang,* v.[1]]
peremo, mortifico, neco, to sle [slay]
obio, morior, to dy
fameo, exurio, famesco, to hunggur
scitio, to thurst
macero, make lene
maceo, be lene
macesco, wex lene [grow lean]
marcesco, begyn to vanys [*OED, vanish,* 2., disappear by decaying, coming to an end]
racionor, to rekyng [reckon]
excaterisco, to scalde
ianitor, appadio, to leue [leave, depart]
acillo, waxe sowre
marito, nubo, marito, disponso, sponso, duco, coniugo, to wede [wed; *marito* repeated]

Folio 331a

[Treatise on verbs of the first conjugation; only the following verbs are glossed in English.]
libo, to taste or offre
cibo, to fede
conglobo, wynde togedir
aproprobo, to [ ] for gode [*aproprobo,* error for *approbo*; to ( ), blank space on line]
inprobo, id est falcitatem osctendere, to preve fals
subo, est porcoris, to bremyn [not in *MED*; error for *brennyn*? *subo,* be in heat (of sows; *MED, brennen,* 5a. (a), of an emotion: to be fervent]
turbo, id est impedire, to lettyn [prevent]
acerbo, to make bitter or sower

Folio 331b

limbo, to hemme a clothe
sebulbo, allium decorticare, to pele garlic
vnco, make a crooke
adunco, make croked
ructo, to syng with a trompe [comic gloss; *ructo*, belch; see fol. 146a]
cortico, to takyn of barke [*of*, off]
ecliptico, to makyn merkor de faūc, [indecipherable abbreviation, perhaps relating to alchemy; *merkor, mercury*]
fisco, to takyn in to the kyngis hand
opaco, make derke
pico, to cleme with pich [*MED, clemen*, plaster (with pitch)]
epico, pike a bone
impudico, make vn chaste

Folio 332a

suplico, make a fold
plico, to fold
implico, folde in
applico, folde to and ryue to lande [*ryue, OED, rive*, v.[2], to arrive, to land]
replico, folde ageyn
multiplico, make manyfold
rudico, to takyn rote [take root]
eradico, draw vp rote
silabico, to spelyn [spell, name letters in word or syllable]
nigrifico, make blac
thurifico, to ensensyn [cense]
occo, to clotty lond [*MED, clotten*, break up clods, harrow; error for *clottyn*?]
taco, make fowl [make foul; *taco*, error for *caco*, besmear with ordure]
paco, to pay money
voco, calle
prouoco, to prouokyn

Folio 332b

seco, kerve
receco, shere ageyn
toxico, to poysyn
sacrifico, to halowe
amplifico, make large
exerpico, to harow
mico, to shyne
emico, splender
frico, to frotyn [rub]
mico, to meycrommys [not in *MED, OED*; *mico* can mean the finger game played in Italy today as *mora*]
ofunico, wede corn
vendico, to calenge [challenge]
pedico, to stampe [stamp (foot)]
fortifico, forte facere, make strong

Folio 333a

claudico, to halten [limp]
honorifico, to honowry [honor; error for *honowryn*?]
excodico, to grubbe [*MED, grubben*, c., dig up (a tree by its roots)]
purifico, make clene
pullefico, make blake
vmarico, make bitter
mollifico, make softe
loco, settyn to hire [put out a contract to have a thing done]
disloco, put out of hire
ratifico, to wouchsaf [vouchsafe]
ceco, make blynde
visco, take with lyme [snare with birdlime; *viscus, -um*, birdline]

Folio 333b

certifico, make certeyn
vincido, to vengin [avenge]
falco, to mowe
iudico, to demyn [judge]
sicco, to ereyn [error for *dreyn*, dry]
confisco, to exchetyn in to þe kyngis hondis [*exchetyn*, escheat (forfeit)]

conuisco, take with lym [snare with birdlime (see fol. 333a, *visco*)]
lubrico, to slivern [*OED*, *slive*, v.[2], cause to slip]
prenostico, significare, to mene
mestifico, make sory [make sorry; *m(a)estus*, sorrowful, dejected]
inculco, blame or to wite [*wite* blotted; *wite* = blame; OED, *wite*, v.[1]]
nidifico, to make nestis
communico, to comown and oselen [*comown*, take communion, the sacrament; *MED*, *houselen*, administer or partake of the sacrament; *MED* does not record the sp. *os*-]
excommunico, to cursen
fabrico, to forgyn

Folio 334a

vilifico, make fowle
mastifico, chewyn
muco, to sonyte þe nose [*sonyte*, error for *snot*; *OED*, *snot*, v. 2., blow the nose; first cit., sixteenth century]
castifico, make chaste
sulco, make a forowe
abdico, to geyn sey
tacifico, pacificare, be styll
scarifico, to garse [*MED*, *garsen*, scarify, in medicine]
circumdo, circuire, to gone abought [go about]
pessimdo, to castyn down and defowlyn
hbundo, to make plentewouse [plenteous; *hbundo*, error for *habundo*]
redundo, to ebbyn [ebb]
fecundo, make plente
vado, waden [wade]
nudo, make naked
laudo, collaudo, preysyn
nodo, knytte
denodo, vnkytte [error for *vnknytte*]
sedo, stawnche
solido, make sadde [settle; *OED*, *sad*, 2., settled, steadfast, firm]
subsolido, to trede or make sadde
rotundo, make rownde
fundo, slyng or sette

Folio 334b

sudo, to swetyn [sweat]
exherido, disherityn
lupido, stawnchyn
mundo, make clene
incrudo, make rawe
emendo, make amendis
madido, make moyst
cordido, make foule
formido, dredyn
grauido, to make with chydde [error for *chylde*; see fol. 352a, *grauo*]
dilucido, shewyn
pedo, gon on fote
discordo, to discorde
limpido, make clere

Folio 335a

largo, largum facere, make large
musido, to makyn mowlyd [word blotted; *mucidus*, moldy; *MED*, *moulen*, grow moldy]
beo, make holy
creo, to makyn a thyng of nought [create, make something of nothing; Varro (6.81) argues that *creo* derives by metathesis from *cerno* ("I see"): when something is created, then finally it is seen]
screo, to spete [spit]
nauseo, to brake [*MED*, *braken*, vomit]
calseo, to hosyn and shoyn [provide, fit, with hose and shoes]

Folio 335b

offo, to make soppis [sops, bread soaked in water, wine, etc.]
stuffo, to stove or calle a hawke

[*stove*, *OED*, *stow*, int., used by falconer to call a hawk back to his fist; first cit., sixteenth century]
purgo, make clene
ligo, bynde
indigo, limite
vestigo, to seke [seek, track, trace]
rigo, make moyste
prolongo, purloyned [error for *prolonged*]
oblongo, to make alonge
litigo, to stryve
fatigo, make wery
mitigo, swagin [assuage]
iugo, to ȝokyn bestis [yoke beasts]
subnigo, to vnder putten
profligo, turmentyn
instigo, to baytyn and entysyn [*baytyn*, *MED*, *baiten*, 2. (b), incite]
castigo, chastisyn

Folio 336a

nego, to geynseyn [gainsay, deny]
fumico, smekyn or rekyn [smoke]
segrego, partyn [separate]
subligo, vndirbyndyn
deuulgo, schewyn
grengo, take trwce [make a truce; *OED* records the idiom *take truce*]
rugo, make wrynkyld
corrugo, wrynkelyn togeder
elargo, make large
rogo, to praye [ask]
interrogo, petere, to aske

Folio 336b

prestigio, to wichyn [*OED*, *witch*, v., practice witchcraft]
deuio, to gon out of the wey
nuncio, to sey message
abrenuncio, to for sake
sacio, fille
ascio, ascias facere, make sponys [spoons]
fascio, fascia ligare, to swath [*OED*, *swathe*, v., bind]
putacio, to bocche [*MED*, *bocchen*, v., (1), swell]
somno, to dremyn
diuorcio, to part matrimony
excorio, to hydyn [skin, remove hide]
manubro, to make an haste [*haste* not in *MED* in any appropriate sense; *manubro* suggests "sleeve" (*manubrium*); *Promptorium parvulorum* (col. 247) has "speyre = manubium (manulium), opening of a dress or garment"]
capicio, to don on hode [hood; *on*, error for *an*? *don on* is redundant]
spolio, to spoile
vario, to make diuers [vary]

Folio 337a

leuio, to make lyght
exauxinigio, to make fatte
bullo, to selyn [seal (with wax)]
stillo, to droppyn [fall as drops]
sorbillo, to sowpe [sop, absorb]
sigillo, to selyn [seal (with wax)]
assolo, to turne to erthe [*to*, error for *the*?]
girgillo, wynden
lallo, soke mylke
titillo, to waggen
tatillo, to tykyll
catello, to mewte [*MED*, *meuten*, v. (2), of a cat, to mew]
vibrillo, to wegge [appar. = wag; see *titillo* above]
decollo, to smyght of the nekke [*of*, off]

Folio 337b

fibilo, to botten [button]
calculo, to reken
maculo, to soylyn [soil, make dirty]
exulo, to be outlawde
colo, purgare, to clence
volo, to flee [fly]

dolo, to thwite [*OED*, *thwite*, cut down; *dolo* suggests cut with an ax]
anclo, laborare, to pante [gasp; *anclo, laborare* suggest working as a domestic; however, *anclo* may be an error for *anelo*, *anhelo*]
amplo, make large
sello, make sadellis
stimulo, to prykkyn
simulo, to make lyke
millo, suere, to ȝarke [*OED*, *yark*, prepare]
reuelo, to shewe
vigilo, to wakyn [be wakeful]
mutilo, to meymyn
foculo, to kyndelyn

Folio 338a

affulo, palpitare, to femyl [fumble; cf. fol. 343a, *palpo*]
fullo, to walke clothe [*walke*, *OED*, *walk*, v.[2], beat cloth]
commulo, to hepynne [heap (up)]
balo, to blete as a shepe
gratillo, kakelyn as a henne
vlulo, to yellyn
bentulo, to wenowyn corne [*wenowyn*, winnow]
vidulo, cum vidula ludere, to fydylle
indulo, indulas facere, to make augurs of a boke [to tell fortunes by selecting a random page (?); *OED* records no such meanings for *augur* until the sixteenth and seventeenth centuries; *Promptorium parvulorum* (col. 407): "seny = sign, token of a boke (indula)"]
rebello, to fytyn ageyn
celo, to hele a grave [*MED*, *hele*, v. (2), cover, conceal, roof; *celo*, hide; thus the sense is to cover over a grave]
vallo, to be sege [besiege; however, *vallo*, defend]
serculo, to wede corn

Folio 338b

sintillo, to sparkyllyn
flo, sufflo, blowe
mugilo, stertere, to rought [*OED*, *rout*, v.[1], snore]
conflo, to welle to gedere
anclo, furari, to stelyn [steal; *anclo*, be a servant, perhaps error for *an(h)elo*, which could imply desiring, eagerly grasping for]
opilo, obstruere, obstupare, to stoppyn [stop, obstruct]
obulo, to shote brode [*MED*, *brode*, wide; no phrase involving shooting]
coaculo, to crudden to geder [curd together, coagulate]
rumello, to schakyn on hors [bounce on horseback?]
vacillo, to waggen [*OED*, *wag*, totter, oscillate]
excillo, to wexyn sowre

Folio 339a

pipulo, to crye as a fesaunte
panpulo, to cry as a pecoke
strangulo, to woryin [*OED*, *worry*, 1., strangle]
tuculo, cry as a cukkow [*tuculo*, error for *cu-*?]
fugillo, smyte fyre with an yren [strike fire (from flint) with an iron]
congelo, frese togeder
degelo, thawe
degulo, to swowne [swoon (?); *degulo*, "swallow"; perhaps *swowyn*, which *Promptorium parvulorum* (col. 471) equates with *bulbio*, to make noise as water does in rushing down a precipice]
septuplo, make seuenfold
octuplo, make eyte fold
decuplo, make ten folde
instralo, sette stelis in asty [set stiles in a (pig) sty; *OED* records sp. *stele*]
tutelo, defendere, to defendeyn

vinculo, scaturire, to spryng [Lat. indicates that the Eng. is a pun: (1) catch in a snare (*springe*); (2) spring (as water)]
vstulo, cremare, to synge [singe]

Folio 339b

clamo, cry
como, to kymbe [comb]
fimo, fimum facere, spred muke [spread dung; *MED*, *muk*, human or animal excrement]
ramo, sprede branchis
limo, purgare cum lima, to folen [file; *MED* records no such sp., see fol. 318b, *wayle*]
peripsimo, to paryn [pare, peel; *peripsimo*, peel off]
congelimo, to stal [urinate (?); *OED*, *stale*, v.[1] (said of horses or cattle)]
fumo, to reke [smoke]

Folio 340a

infirmo, debilitare, to make seke
deplumo, pluk of fethers [*of*, off]
cremo, brannyn [burn; *MED* records no such sp.]
camio, make in a barnak [put (a horse) into a snaffle; *MED*, *bernak*, snaffle]
fulmo, conguere, sethen [boil]
fleobotomo, to betebowld [not in *MED*; probably error for *lete blowd*, as Lat. indicates]
squamo, disquamo, to scalyn a fissh
grumo, dirugere, equitare, to grate
no, natare, swymme
trano, ouerswymmyn
sano, helyn
mano, fluere, to ren as water
emano, renne out

Folio 340b

sanno, sanam facere, to make a mow [make a face, ridicule; *MED*, *moue*, n. (2), *maken moues*, laugh, ridicule]
signo, to markyn
resigno, to resignyn vp [*OED*, *resign*, v., 2., give up, make over, abandon]
assigno, to assynyn
festino, to hye [hie, hasten]
propino, potum dare, to byrlyn [*MED*, *birlen*, v. (1), serve drink]
diuino, to devinen
sono, to ryngyn
corono, to crownyn
grano, to take corn
ordino, to ordeyn
condono, to geven
sono, to chymyn or knyllyn [knell]
semino, to sow
damno, to damnyn
refreno, to with drawe
cachynno, to makyn a mow [see *sanno* above]
occiteno, to poynt vpwarde

Folio 341a

[p]arrytino, to poynt downward
discranino, to shedyn [shed (hair, as *discranino* indicates]
conglutino, to swelowe [swallow]
inclino, to bow
combino, to bynden to geder
pampino, to sprede on leuys [spread leaves; see fol. 342a, *pampino*]
fulmino, to lyghten [refers to lightning]
suppino, to lygge grovlyng [lie groveling; *MED*, *groveling*, face downward]
resepino, to ly wydeopyn
veneno, texicare, to wevyn [weave]
conglutino, glutino, to glowche [glue; *MED* records no sp. *-che*]

buccino, to trumpe [blow a trumpet]
compagino, knette to geder
cereno, make clere
ameno, make delitable
freno, to brydell
effreno, take of brydell [*of,* off]
rumino, chewyn or codyn [chew cud; *MED, cud,* n., records no related verb]
dapino, to feden
depampino, to blade [*MED, bladen,* strip leaves from a plant]

Folio 341b

cacumino, to make coppid [top, take off the top; *MED, cop,* top, n.; records no related verb]
lumino, to lite
grandino, to hayle [hail, storm]
erugino, to rub of the rust [*of,* off]
determino, determyn
fortuno, deme wordis [interpret words, as a fortune-teller; no such sense in *MED*]
alieno, relegare, to flemne [*MED, flemen,* v. (1), banish, exile]
agino, festinare, hyen [hie, hasten]
sagino, make fat
adno, swemme to

Folio 342a

antelucano, ryse be fore day
conglutino, swalow and to knyt to gedere
inclino, bowe
combino, bynde togedere
pampino, to sprede out leuys [spread leaves; see fol. 341a, *pampino*]
dapino, pascere, fede
subforoino, to vndergirde
infortuno, to mke vnhappy [*mke,* error for *make*]
habeno, to hold þe rayn of a brydell
pectino, to kembe [comb]
lacuno, to krokyn [*MED, croken,* curve; *lacuno,* hollow out, fret, pit]
pedano, make a wampy [*OED, vamp,* sock; records sp. *wampe; vamp* also = part of a boot or shoe]
pagumino, sprede out leuys [spread leaves; see *pampino* above and fol. 341a]

Folio 342b

rebino, to falowe londe [*falowe,* plow]
lixino, boyle
fortuno, deme wordis [see fol. 341b; this entry begins a series of repeated entries]
agino, festinare, to hyen

Folio 343a

sagino, make fat
acino, to tre[?]th [tread(?)]
adnno, swymmyn to
antelucano, rise be fore day
discrimino, diuidere, schede þe heved [*schede, OED, shed,* v., 2., part (the hair)]
culpo, to blame
palpo, to grope [touch, handle with the hands; cf. fol. 338a, *femyl*]
zelotipo, to wex iolys [jealous]
concrepo, blame

Folio 343b

apocap, to cut of the ende [*apocap,* error for -po, -pe?; *of,* off]
alapo, to buffet [strike]
ocupo, to ocupye
scopo, swepe
ca[u]soro, to plete [plead (before a court)]
exploro, insydiari, to spize [not in *OED*; Lat. indicates the sense as "spy"]
roro, to dewe [bedew, fall as dew]

Folio 344a

honoro, to onowre
equiparo, equare, make evene
sero, sera claudere, to loke [lock]
aro, ere lond [plow]

Folio 344b

conlaro, make yoyfull [joyful; followed by *exillaro idem*]
mensuro, mesure
farro, to sho a hors [*sho,* shoe]
ferrus, an hors sho
incarcero, to prisone [imprison]
placero, male loqui, to blabre [*MED, blaberen,* speak incoherently; but Lat. suggests "speak ill of"]
altero, to chaunge
vulnero, to woundyn
cupparo, pannis rugare, to frunce cloþis [*frunce, MED, frouncen,* wrinkle, pleat]
coroboro, make stronge
verbero, percutere, to betyn
perforo, penetrare, to hole [perforate]

Folio 345a

spiro, anelitum capere, to take onde [*OED, onde,* 4., breath]
giro, to wirle abought [whirl about; *giro,* altered from *gipo*]
regiro, turne a geyne
latro, to barke [bark (as a dog)]
oblatro, barke ageyne
cribro, to syfte
excribro, to syuite out of harnes [*syuite,* not in *OED*; appar. = "sift" (remove a man or horse from harness [armor])]
glomero, wyndyn a clwue [clew, ball of yarn]
inpetro, purchace
genero, to getyn [beget]
degenero, gon out of kynde [nature; act unnaturally]
vxoro, to wedde a wyfe
preposterioro, sett before þat was be hynde
recupero, recouer

Folio 345b

suspiro, suspirium facere, to seye [sigh]
numero, to nowmbre
remunero, to reward
stercoro, fimare, to moke [muck, spread dung]
tenero, teneris facere, make tendre
terebro, terebro perforare, to bore with a wymble [gimlet, auger]
lacero, to tere
macero, macerum facere, make lene
pignoro, pignus ponere, to ley a wedde [*OED, wed,* sb., *pledge* (as a pawn)]
maturo, maturum facere, make rype
sepero, to departyn [divide]
minoro, make lesse
alabro, cum alabro operari, to rele [reel, wind up (as wool)]

Folio 346a

libro, trucinare, to wey [weigh]
obumbro, vmbram facere, make shadowe
vibro, to brawnche [brandish; *MED* records the sp. *braunchin*]
serro, cum serra perforare, to saw a tree
tenebro, make darke
latero, cast vper the side [*vper,* error for *vpon*]
redintegro, make hol ageyn [*hol,* whole]
prospero, make happy or sely [happy]

fragro, redolere, to smel sote [sweet]
invetero, make old
recalcitro, retro calcitare, to wynd vp be hynde
paupero, make pore
obturo, obstruere, to stoppe [obstruct]
spero, to hopyn [hope]
exaggero, to gader on hepe [heap]

Folio 346b

capistro, to halter [tie with a halter]
accuro, to thanke
balistro, to schete with an a weblast [*MED*, *arblast*, weapon for discharging quarrels, stones, etc.; records sp. *arblast*]
floro, flores spergere, to springe flowres [*OED*, *springe*, *spring*, has no sense of causing flowers to grow or of strewing flowers]
haustro, humectare, make moyst

Folio 347a

liro, arare, sultare, to make forow [furrow]
depuro, deformare, to defowlyn [befoul, deform]
scabro, scaturire, to spring [spring (as water)]
zelero, to do felonye [followed by *conzelero idem est*]
tabero, tumere, to swell
refrigero, to kelyn [cool]
rostro, cum rostro percutere, make sharpe
deuoro, to swelwe [swallow]
crasso, make fatte [followed by *incrasso idem est*]
casso, to woyde or wast [empty, or lay waste]
succurso, to trotte
potisso, potare, to sowpyn [sup, dine]
spisso, make thikke
virisso, to pryve [deprive]

Folio 347b

fesso, make wery
asso, to rost [roast]
acuso, to be wreye [accuse, betray]
recuso, refutere, to forsakyn
excuso, to excusyn
equepenso, eque pensare, to wey evyn [to deliberate, "weigh evenly"]

Folio 348a

dempso, densum facere, to make yik [error for þik]
gipso, cum gipse limire, to dawbe
nato, nare, swymme
dilato, make brode
fato, euenire, to distayn be wordis [*MED*, *destinen*, foreordain]
crato, scalpere, to schrape and clawe [*schrape*, scrape, scratch]

Folio 348b

[u]ito, to fle [flee; followed by *euito idem est*]
cito, to somwn [summon]
incito, instigare, to entysyn
dito, make riche
ablacto, to wenn a child fro mylke
cogito, to thynkyn [followed by *excogito idem est*]
agito, minare, to dryve
fugito, vitare, to fle
vellito, to draw vpe by the rote
precipto, sternere, bete down

Folio 349a

planto, to impe [*MED*, *impen*, to plant]
latito, to derkyn
roto, rotam vertere, to turne a whele

compito, to telle [count]
imputo, to wyte [blame; followed by *reputo idem est*; see fol. 333b, *inculco*]
deputo, to geve in kepyng
repto, frequenter repere, to crepe

Folio 349b

optento, adquirere, to purchace
detento, retinere, to with holde
contento, contentum facere, make payde [MED, *paien*; *maken paied*, to content, please]
intento, minari, to threte [threaten]
distento, frequenter distendere, to sprede out
demento, insanum facere, to make wode [mad, insane; followed by *dimento idem est*]
lento, vnbend for to make croked [*vnbend*, perhaps an error for *bend*]
sto, to stonde
ossito, to grone [groan]
sternuto, to nese [sneeze]

Folio 350a

incito, instigare, to chasyn [chase, but see the same Lat. words on fol. 348b]
vasto, vastum facere, make large or wast [enlarge or lay waste; prob. not "make vast," *OED*, *vast*, first cit. late sixteenth century]
tempto, to asayn [try]
commilito, militare, to stryvyn [struggle]
equito, to ryde
humito, humidum facere, make moyst
suscito, to reyse vp

Folio 350b

attracto, trahere, vecco, to bere
dormito, to slumberyn
veto, inhibere, prohibere, to for bede
certo, contendere, to stryve
recito, to rehersyn [recite]
iacto, to castyn or bostyn [throw or boast]
esito, dubitare, to dowtyn
cespito, stumbelyn
locupleto, make ryche
porto, bere
inporto, bere in
apporto, bryng to
asporto, bere awey
reporto, brynge aȝen
egroto, wexen seke [grow sick]
abrepto, to gyn to go [begin to go (?); *gyn* may be the weak auxiliary with present meaning: *MED*, *ginnen*, 3. b (b)]

Folio 351a

arieto, hurtyn as a ram [hurt (butt) like a ram]
ceculto, make blynde
singulto, sobbe
decosto, don awey a rybbe
deserto, make wylde or wast
angusto, make streyte or narowe
cocto, to sethen [boil]
infelicito, to maken vnsely [unhappy]
comictere, confundere, refutere, for to sake [error for *to for sake*]

Folio 351b

gutto, to droppyn [drop (as water)]
degutto, droppe a down
sugicito, to vnder sitte
lato, make brode [followed by *dilato idem est*]
nuto, to berkyn [error for *beckyn*, nod with the head]
onusto, to charge [load]
deonusto, to discharge
intempesto, molestare, to greve [vex, oppress (often by military ac-

tion)]
pnto, to peynte [*pnto*, error for *pinto*; followed by *pingito idem est*]
susprinto, to vnder wene [undervalue]
sagitto, sagittam emittere, to shote [shoot (an arrow)]
prorito, provocare, to calle foryt [error for *forth*(?)]
quirito, populum alloqui, to reysyn the people [arouse the people, incite to action]
solicito, solitum esse, comouere, make besy [busy]
sputo, streate, to spytte
tuto, tutum facere, make syker [safe]
tristo, tristem facere, make sory [followed by *contristo idem est*]
turbulento, make hevy [disturbed, sad]
verrito, verrere, to wrote [*OED*, *wroot*, root, (as swine)]
prigrito, pigrum esse vel fieri, to wex slowe [*OED*, *slow*, 2. b., characterized by sloth; *prigrito*, error for *pigrito*]
exagito, to dryve

Folio 352a

sarmento, to shrede [*OED*, *shred*, 1., prune (trees, bushes)]
puncto, pansare, to make restyng [at rest (?); growing rancid (rest, adj.) (?); Lat. suggests puncturing, making an aperture, opening out; see next entry]
cauo, make holowe
grauo, greve or make with shild [error for *child*; the scribe makes a similar error on fol. 344b; *greve*, *MED* does not record the sense of impregnate]
lauo, lotum vel lautum, washe
clauo, clauo ingere, to nayle
leuo, extollere, to ryse [*OED*, *rise*, trans., 27a, rear or breed; 27. b., raise to life; both are marked *rare*]
priuo, cassere, to foe doun [not in *MED*; perhaps error for *for don*; *OED*, *fordo*, 5., undo, bring to nought; Lat. suggests a meaning like "deprive"]
conuiuo, conuiuium facere, make a fest [feast]
adaquo, to water
equo, make even

Folio 352b

visuiuo, passe ouere twys [twice; *visuiuo*, evidently an error for *bis-*]
euo, wax wood [grow (go) mad]
liquo, melte
niuo, niuigere, to snowe
proteruo, proteruium facere, make wicked
laxo, to vndon [undo, loosen]
relaxo, relese
malaxo, knede
mataxo, to hechyll [*MED*, *hechelen*, card flax]
pexo, to kembe [comb]
pandoxo, to brewe
coraxo, to garse [*MED*, *garsen*, scarify (in medicine)]
elixo, to seþe [boil; followed by *torquere lixo*]
the sqwyrell [squirrel; no Lat.; immediately followed by next entry]
wasche brenne [wash bran; followed by *messis in aqua*]
taxo, clamare ad modum rane, to crowde as a padoge [paddock, frog; *crowde*, *MED*, *crouden*, v. (3), croak]

Folio 353a

pretaxo, palmitare, to bargayn
hyo, to galpyn [*MED*, *galpen*, yawn, gape]
thesaurizo, to gader tresoure

alapizo, to buffetyn [buffet, strike]
baptizo, to crystyn
excaturizo, to scald

Folio 353b

citherizo, to harpe
calamiso, to pype in a rede or to thakke [thatch (two distinct meanings in this gloss)]
preconizo, comendare, crye os a bedill [*MED, bidel,* one who makes an announcement, in the service of a lord, etc.; *os,* as]
taratantarizo, to sifte mele

[Brief section on deponent verbs follows.]

procor, aliquid petere, to wowe [woo, petition]
precor, to prey [ask]
adulor, to glose [flatter]

Folio 354a

frugor, to stele [steal; *frugor,* perhaps an error for *furor*]
aduiniculor, metor, to mete [measure]
machinor, to cumpace [*MED, compassen,* devise a plan]
execro, to werie [*OED, wary,* v., curse]
miror, stupere, to wondour
palustror, to wrestell
venor, to hunt
sciscitor, to speren [*OED, speer,* v.[1], to put a question]

Folio 354b

ringo, to grynne
culmino, to thacche
culmen, a thecche
malaxo, to knede

Folios 355a ff.

Include treatises on rhetoric, neuter words, and a collection of hymns, written as prose, including the *Pange lingua gloriosi* of both Saint Thomas and Fortunatus.

Folio 385a

cirographus, a wrytyng apon, *id est* tombe [marginal scribble, in a later hand]

INDEX OF ENGLISH WORDS AND PHRASES

Numbers after entries refer to folios of the manuscript. Included are proper names referred to in the bracketed commentary.
Note: Folios 302-307a are bound out of order; in this edition the order of the manuscript is preserved, and no attempt is made to reorder the folios.

A

B

C

E

F

G, ȝ

H

L

M

N

Q

R

S

V (including vocalic v)

W

Y (see also ȝ, I)